Favorite
Dog Hikes
IN AND AROUND
Los Angeles

**SPOTTED
DOG PRESS**®

BISHOP 🐾 CALIFORNIA

SPOTTED DOG PRESS®

ISBN Number: 1-893343-11-1
Published by Spotted Dog Press, Inc.
Box 1721, Bishop, CA 93515-1721
Call 800-417-2790 for a free catalog
Order online at www. SpottedDogPress.com

SECOND EDITION 2003
Book design & layout by Spotted Dog Press, Inc.
No part of this book may be reproduced in any form, or by any electronic,
mechanical or other means without permission in writing from the publisher.
Photographs by Wynne Benti unless otherwise noted.
Canine boot design and illustrations ©1995-2004 by Terry Austin
Spotted Dog Press is a registered trademark of Spotted Dog Press, Inc.
Cover: Wynne Benti and Ruby by Andy Zdon
Back cover: Andy Zdon with Syd, admires Mt. Baldy by the author
Insets, top to bottom: Arroyo Seco; Cerro Negro and Mt. Lukens; Hermosa Greenbelt;
Kim keeps warm with layers in winter, photos by the author
Opposite: The author on the approach to Panamint Butte, Death Valley by Andy Zdon
KoKo, abandoned and rescued from Death Valley, adopted from the Big Pine Shelter,
photo by the author

Benti, Wynne,
Favorite Dog Hikes: in and around Los Angeles/by Wynne Benti--2nd ed.
     p. cm.
Includes bibliographical references (p.) and index.
1-893343-11-1 (alk. paper)
1. Dog Hiking--Los Angeles--Guidebooks. 2. Dog Hiking--California--Guidebooks. I. Title.

Produced and printed in the United States of America

About the author

Wynne Benti (*Climbing Mt. Whitney*), grew up in the Valley, attending grammar school in Encino and high school in Studio City. An avid surfer, Benti spent most of her days after high school at Malibu's Third Point. Daughter of a retired news anchorman, Benti was right there as her father covered some of the most sensational stories in the City of Los Angeles. A graduate of the University of California at Davis and Art Center College of Design in Pasadena, Benti worked for many years in network television before moving to the Eastern Sierra with her husband.

Benti has climbed more than 600 mountains in the southwest including the highpoints of the San Gabriel, San Bernardino, San Jacinto and Santa Monica Mountains. An avid paddler, she paddled her canoe on the Yukon (from Whitehorse to Dawson), Green, Colorado and other rivers. Considered an authority on hiking with dogs, Benti cofounded the K9 Committee of the Sierra Club's largest chapter in Los Angeles. Her dogs, k.d. and Syd, adopted from the East Valley Animal Shelter, were awarded official Mascot Status in the Hundred Peaks Section for climbing twenty-five peaks in the local mountains. Benti has received awards for volunteer community service including the Gerald L. Phillippe award from General Electric and a letter of commendation from Mayor James Hahn, then City Attorney of Los Angeles, for her work on the preservation of the natural stretches of the Los Angeles River.

That's my momma!

A NOTE ABOUT SAFETY

Hiking can be a risky sport associated with many hazards including but not limited to those mentioned in this book: adverse weather conditions, snake bites, insect bites, animal bites, dehydration, heat stroke or exhaustion, hypothermia, slipping, falling or other types of injury as well as potential contact with unsavory characters and canines. The hikes in this book have been rated for difficulty. Please note the difficulty rating of each hike and do not hike above yours or your dog's skill level! There is no substitute for experience, skill, knowledge of safety procedures and common sense!

The publisher and author of this guide makes no representation as to the safety of any hiking or driving route described herein. At the time of this printing, route descriptions were accurate. However, conditions are constantly changing and it is recommended that you contact the supervising park agency or consult available map information to find out about current conditions before you hike.

TABLE OF CONTENTS

ACKNOWLEDGEMENTS

This trail guide was written for everyone who wants to get out of town for a day, to hike the trails or experience the mountains and valley grasslands with their favorite canine friend. It is a guide to some of the prettiest and most natural parkland trails, in and around Los Angeles, where dogs are welcome. New to this edition are walks in the South Bay including Palos Verdes, and what I like to call *urban walks* along the bluffs and marinas of San Pedro and Long Beach.

The United States Forest Service Angeles National Forest and National Park Service Santa Monica Mountains National Recreation Area provided the author with a wealth of information.

To my dedicated readers and their dogs, Danny Gray and Mushie, Eddy Berg and Megan, Chris Lee and her pup, Andy Zdon and the girls, Breann Benti and Lyla, Edmund Bentivengo's BooBoo and Beanie, Julie Rush and Tilly, the Angeles Chapter of the Sierra Club's K9 Committee and all of the dogs and people kind enough to let me snap their pictures, thank you.

Our dogs were eager companions on the trail: up at dawn, hiking until sunset, scouting, sniffing and exploring: Syd and k.d. adopted from the East Valley Animal Shelter on Sherman Way; Ruby, a red cattle dog pup adopted outside Carson City, Nevada, and KoKo-puff, a small Chow-cattle dog mix, found starving and abandoned in Death Valley at only seven weeks old, rescued from the Inyo County Animal Shelter in Big Pine, California. My dear sweet husband, Richard, thank you for everything.

To everyone who provides a good, caring home to a homeless shelter dog, cat or other companion pet, thank you. Love, access to medical care, good food and a cozy, safe bed: it doesn't take much for us to make a difference in their lives.

*"Mr. Young and the
Indians were asleep, and so,
I hoped, was Stickeen;
but I had not gone a dozen rods
before he left his bed
in the tent and came boring
through the blast after me.
That a man should welcome
storms for their exhilarating
music and motion…
…is reasonable enough;
but what fascination could there be in such
tremendous weather for a dog?"*

John Muir, Stickeen: The Story of a Dog • 1909

THE HEROIC DOG

INTRODUCTION

In 1880, naturalist John Muir discovered firsthand what a great companion a dog was in the wilderness while on an expedition to explore Alaska's Inside Passage. Despite objections by Muir and others, one of expedition members brought along his dog, a small terrier mix named "Stickeen" after the Stikine River across from Wrangell Island in what is now the Tongass National Forest. With its headwaters in Canada, the Stikine is the fastest flowing navigable river in America.

As far as everyone on Muir's expedition was concerned, the tiny Stickeen beared no resemblance to the mighty river. The small dog was seen only as a burden, something else to hamper the progress of serious exploration and study.

One morning, before his companions were awake, Muir dressed and left the tent in the midst of a storm, to experience the beauty of the wilderness. He wrote:

"Mr. Young and the Indians were asleep, and so, I hoped, was Stickeen; but I had not gone a dozen rods before he left his bed in the tent and came boring through the blast after me. That a man should welcome storms for their exhilarating music and motion and go forth to see God making landscapes is reasonable enough; but what fascination could there be in such tremendous weather for a dog?"

No storm was too fierce, no river current too fast, no mountain canyon or crag too treacherous to deter the little dog from walking along side his human companions. Stickeen surprised everyone on that Alaskan adventure with his fortitude, courage and will.

The first person to fly over both the north and south poles was American aviator and explorer, Admiral Richard E. Byrd, leader of many notable polar and transatlantic flights. Accompanying Byrd was his small terrier, Igloo, who shared notably in his master's accomplishments.

Susan Butcher moved to Alaska from Massachusetts when she was twenty, living alone for nine years, her closest neighbor forty miles away. She and her team of sled dogs went on to win the 1,152 mile Iditarod race four times braving one hundred mph winds, seventy degree below zero temperatures, and the frozen Alaskan terrain with its inherent challenges. "You have to be selfless in your dedication to your dogs" she said in an interview to the Los Angels Times. "When you come into a checkpoint, although there may be a wood stove to warm your feet by, you stay outside; you take care of your dogs, get them bedded down and fed. It may take three hours. Then you can go and have your fifteen minutes inside, and then it's time to go and check your dogs, massage them down and get ready to go again. I might get a catnap."

Workers, shepherds, protectors, rescuers, companions; the relationship between us and our dogs dates back thousands of years. The DNA of dogs and wolves is almost identical, but somewhere along the line, one chose begging the scraps of a meal around the comfort of a human campfire while the other preferred the freedom to roam, to hunt, and live apart from humans.

In the cradle of civilization archaeologists uncovered a burial: a human skeleton tenderly holding the bones of a dog to its breast. In the Arctic, archaeologists date the relationship between dogs and the Inuit back at least one thousand years through fossilized evidence, but know the two have been together for much longer.

Though my pound pups have not yet made history, they walk along the trail with me wherever I go, whenever the law lets them. They know the pair of shoes that means a walk is imminent. Starting at the crack of dawn, until the collar and the leash come off the wall they listen for keys words: "Walk." "W" "Do you want to . . ." They watch my eyes, my movements. They stomp and sigh impatiently. With the leash in her mouth, KoKo tugs me along from the kitchen door to the car while Ruby patiently wanders alongside.

They won't be navigating crevasse fields in Alaska or searching for victims in the debris left behind by a fallen building like their notable canine contemporaries. Their adventure will be a day in the beautiful mountains and grasslands of Los Angeles County with their favorite person. They have walked with me through forests of pine, through sycamores and oaks along coastal trails in windswept grasslands. The moment they hop out of the car and feel the dust of the trail beneath their paws, they know to walk, and to keep on walking until they reach the end of the canyon or the mountain top. They love to explore every new trail. Even the old familiar fire road walked a hundred times promises something new each day. They live to smell the chaparral, wander beneath the sycamore trees, to feel the sun warming their fur as they nap atop a San Gabriel mountain summit.

Before the first writing of this book was finished in 1995, fires had swept across the Santa Monicas, again. After the fires, came floods, mudslides, and finally, the 1994 earthquake. There were so many road closures and detours in the year following the earthquake, a drive that once took half an hour by freeway became a navigational adventure. Ironically, the day my husband and I scouted the Latigo Canyon to Castro Crest hike via the Backbone Trail, a sizable 5.3 aftershock swept over the Los Angeles basin. As we walked back down the trail from the oak-covered crest, we ran into an excited couple who asked if we had felt the aftershock. We hadn't felt or seen the ground move all day. Enraptured by the flowers and other trailside odors, our dogs meandered along oblivious to any earth movement. It's just a different story on the trail.

This trail guide includes some of our favorite walks in and around Los Angeles, done time and again with my four dogs. In most hiking guides, dogs are usually mentioned as an afterthought if at all, in the chapter about trail courtesy, the *no* chapter as I like to call it. The *no* chapter is the one about all of the *no* things, what you can and cannot do: *no* littering, *no* smoking on trails, no radios, *no* motorized vehicles and *no* dogs. Those *no* chapters helped inspire the writing of this book, and since most guides are written only for people, there is little information available about trails and parks in and around Los Angeles where dogs are welcome visitors, too.

ANDY AND SYD

POUND PUPS MAKE GREAT HIKING COMPANIONS

I went to the East Valley Animal Shelter on Sherman Way intent on adopting a watch dog. Instead, I found a companion that walked with me on the trail for the next thirteen years of her life. She looked like she could be part Doberman, and a watch dog. Little, shiny black "k.d." was a stray picked up scrounging on the streets of Los Angeles, not a kind place for a homeless dog or cat. Our connection was immediate as her good-natured smile radiated from behind her cage. In all the years I had her, she never once barked at a noise around the house, but she howled with the coyotes and emergency sirens. A sweet dog who loved the mountain trails, k.d. was such a great hiker that a friend nicknamed her the "lean, mean hiking machine." Two months later, I went back to the East Valley Animal Shelter to find a companion for k.d.. Dogs are social creatures and two of them are about as easy to take care of as one.

As days pass at the shelter, the dogs and cats not adopted move along in the hierarchy of cages, from the center to the outside cages and their last chance for adoption before being euthanized. In the outer cages, I found a young Australian cattle dog, the breed immortalized in Mel Gibson's epic MAD MAX movies. She was a blue merle, still cloaked in pup white with black and blue spots. She barely looked at me when I bent down and put my fingers on her cage. A malnourished victim of terrible abuse and neglect with three different kinds of worms, a bloody cough and broken rib, she was a dog with little happiness left. Without lifting her head from crossed paws, her sad eyes followed me from one end of her cage to the other. "I'll take her," I told the attendant. He said to me, as he lifted shy "Syd" from the cage, "She'll be a loyal, good dog. Just give her a chance."

On our way home, through La Tuna Canyon on the backside of the Verdugos, Syd stood on the inside wheel-well of my old truck, her head poised upward next to the open window. As the wind passed across her face, she closed her eyes, an expression of freedom or resignation to a certain fate, I don't know. Perhaps she just loved the smell of the warm wind filled with the pungent scent of chaparral.

For the next 13 years, k.d., Syd, and I chased up and down the mountain trails of the San Gabriels, Los Padres, San Bernardinos, out to the small ranges on the periphery of Joshua Tree, into the Sierra, across the volcanic tablelands of the northern Owens Valley, up to the high peaks of the White Mountains and Granite Peak. We had a new pup by then, a red cattle dog we named "Ruby." k.d. had already taught Ruby the fine arts: begging, rawhide chip thievery and hiding, chewing tissues, unrolling toilet paper rolls, pouncing upon bushes to flush out lizards in the backyard. Syd, suffering from arthritis, followed us as far as the gate where she sat waiting for our return.

We brought one more home from the shelter: KoKo, a small Chow-cattle dog mix. She was abandoned at 5 weeks old in Death Valley, found by a maintenance man at Furnace Creek. A couple living in Death Valley took her in, but after a month drove her to the shelter in Big Pine, California, where they turned their backs and left her. She was so traumatized when she saw them leave, that she started to cry, to scream. Then every time a potential adoptive parent walked by her cage she cried, screamed as if to say, "Don't leave me." By the time we came along the shelter folks called her "the screamer." My husband fell in love with her, and home she came. She had what I call "issues." She suffered from terrible separation anxiety. Most shelter dogs have psychological issues from abusive past experiences with human beings. It may take some time, but with our patience, love, understanding, good food, and a safe bed inside the family home, the demons from their past can be worked out.

Nowadays, plump little old Syd prefers relaxation and singing along with me to musical numbers from "Paint Your Wagon." KoKo and Ruby walk. "k.d." They are my best friends and without them, there would have been little inspiration to write this trail guide. It is my hope that everyone, dog and human alike, who uses this book has as much fun as I do, walking the trails on my favorite dog hikes in and around Los Angeles.

POUND PUP KOKO TACKLES A STEEP TRAIL IN PORTUGUESE BEND

MULTI-USE TRAILS: SHARING THE TRAIL WITH OTHERS

When we first started hiking these trails, most of the parking lots were dirt and empty. It was rare to run into anyone. During the past decade, the trails in this book have grown in popularity as have the ways in which people use them.

Today, we share the trails with other dogs, walkers, runners, hikers, mountain bikers, equestrians, packers and pack animals, fishermen, bird-watchers, hunters, motorcyclists–essentially people of all ages and interests. Include in that lengthy list all of the people we didn't think to mention as well as those who like dogs, those who are afraid of dogs and those who don't like dogs–all very good reasons to keep your dog close to you.

For most of us, leashes are without a doubt, the best way to know where our pets are all the time. My technique of *hands-free leashing*, which requires clipping a rock climbing carabiner to your belt loop or pack belt, then clipping your dog's leash into the carabiner, is a great way to keep your dog next to you and your hands free. In addition, the most important verbal command you can teach your dog for wilderness travel is "come." When you say your dog's name along with that word, your dog should forego all other distractions and return to you at once. In fact, your dog's ability to respond to that one simple command could mean the difference between life and death, on or off-leash. You and your dog can learn these techniques in a group dog obedience class.

Like people, all dogs have individual personalities. Their unique responses to situations along the trail may at times be difficult to predict, on-leash or off. Many times, a dog's worst enemy on the trail, with the exception of rattlesnakes and ticks are unleashed dogs.

A word here about mountain bikers. Some navigate the trails with care and concern, while others do not. We have encountered mountain bikers who come down a trail so quickly and quietly, that we didn't see or hear them until they were right on top of us and our dogs. It is very easy for a person or dog to inadvertently wander into the path of a mountain bike. Be aware of this especially on popular trails. The more you are aware of what's going on around you, the safer and happier you and your dog will be.

OTHER DOGS

You will meet up with other dogs along the trail who share your love of exploring wild places. Like people, dogs will come in an assortment of sizes, shapes and personalities, some friendly, some not so friendly. Eventually, you may even meet up with an alpha dog. This dog must be the top dog above all others, the leader of the pack and will fight until death, literally, to be the leader. Jack London wrote about the alpha behavior of sled dogs during the 1898 Klondike gold rush in his classic stories, *The Call of the Wild* and *White Fang.*

My sister's husband had a male Rottweiler named Bart (who has since passed away from old age). The ancient Roman Army used Rottweilers to guard cattle and protect their camps. Bart loved to

SOCIALIZING ON VETTER MOUNTAIN

hike, but before my sister and her husband married, he spent most of his life in the backyard. Barely socialized, and an alpha male, his primordial instinct was to dominate all other dogs. Not preferring to impose his personality on others, Bart was leashed in public. Unfortunately, this did not keep unleashed dogs from coming over to him and naturally Bart defended his owner. Not all Rottweilers are like Bart. Any pure or mixed breed of dog has its share of alpha and unsocialized personalities.

Once, we encountered a dog and his master in a trailhead parking lot in the Angeles Forest. We had just parked our car when his dog saw our two dogs hanging their heads out the window. While his master yelled a litany of confused, garbled commands with arms a-flailing, the unruly beast camed barreling toward our car and leapt against it in a snarling frenzy. His owner's failure to control him was bad style and gives all of us dog owners a bad reputation.

It is natural for dogs to test other dogs, to find their place in the pack. On leash or off, unless dogs are trained to stay, dogs WILL run over to other dogs. It's a rare dog that's oblivious to the presence of other dogs.

OH BEHAVE! SOCIALIZE YOUR DOG

Socialize your dog at an early age. Get them used to being around other dogs, people and children. A great place to socialize a young dog is at a dog park or obedience class. For about six weeks, dogs and owners are all together learning the basics of good behavior: how to sit, stay, come, and walk on leash. Socializing will help your dog feel comfortable around other canines and with a little obedience training thrown in, should minimize aggressive behavior toward other dogs, people and children.

Only you know your dog. With the knowledge you have of your pet, you should always be prepared to deal with any unexpected situation encountered on the trail.

HANDS-FREE LEASHING

Hands-free leashing is the best way to keep your dog attached to you without having to physically hold a leash. Visit the rock climbing section of your local outdoor retailer and buy a carabiner, unlocking or locking. Recently KMART has stocked small brightly colored carabiners at the checkout stands. Attach the carabiner to a belt loop on your shorts or around the fastened belt of your day pack or fanny pack. Put the end of your dog's nylon leash inside the carabiner and snap it shut.

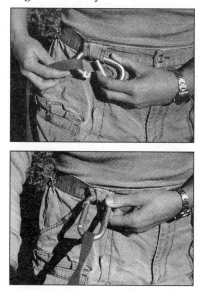

When I wear a day pack, I attach carabiners to my pack's waist belt, then attach one, two or more dogs to my waist on each carabiner. They pull me up the mountain trails, and they love it! It must be that sled dog team thing. I know exactly where they are all the time and can easily reel them in when needed.

HANDS-FREE LEASHING

When traveling southern in California's chaparral country be aware of rattlesnakes. Dogs will pounce on a rattlesnake before you yell "no!" A rattlesnake bite can kill a dog. Dog owners have a great responsibility on and off the trail to always keep their four-legged hiking companions close to them and under control.

PET IDENTIFICATION TAG

My dogs each have two tags on their collars, a license and an engraved identification tag with my name and phone number. ID tags with your dog's name, your name, phone number and address can be ordered in various shapes and clip into the ring on the dog's collar. Call the animal control agency on the tag to ID pet and owner.

WATER, BOWL AND A LEASH!

Water, a lightweight plastic bowl, and a sturdy leash are essential on any hike. Natural water sources in most southland parks and forests are virtually non-existent. I cannot stress the importance of having enough water for you and your dog. When you plan the contents of your day pack consider that water weighs about 1-3/4 pounds per quart, and depending on where you hike, you'll be carrying a day's worth of water for the both of you. Plan walks early in the morning and in the early evening. Be out of the heat of midday. Get an early start for longer hikes and go on cool days.

In a pinch, a plastic lunch bag can double as a make-shift bowl. If you want your pet to carry its own water, purchase a dog pack from an outdoor outfitter, one with good padding on the chest and back straps. Before you leave home, familiarize your dog with its new pack. Put the pack on your dog to get the right fit, then try it with a load. Take your dog for a walk to work out problems before hitting the trail.

Minimum quantities for canine water are listed in under each hike in this book. The recommended amounts are based on the needs of a medium-sized dog weighing about 35 pounds in moderate temperatures (65-70 degrees). Every dog has different needs and it will be up to you to determine how much water your dog will need. Carry at least an extra gallon in your car. Large, collapsible plastic water containers (from 2.5 gallons and up) are available from outdoor equipment stores. Dogs welcome a cold drink of water back at the car after a long, dusty hike.

Never depend on natural water sources for your water supply, even if one is noted on your topo map. Streams can be dry at any time of the year or unfit for human (and canine consumption). People should never drink from any natural, unfiltered water source in the Santa Monica or San Gabriel Mountains, or any other wilderness location in the west. Most streams in California contain bacteria and other stuff that can cause various intestinal ailments, resulting in unpleasant symptoms such as abdominal pain, gas, diarrhea, or worse, necessitating a trip to the emergency room.

One particularly nasty bug known as Giardia Lamblia is found in human and animal waste and contaminates water sources. The microscopic giardia cysts can usually be removed from a water source with the use of a portable water filter, purchased at an outdoor equipment store. Portable water filters are typically used on extended backpacking trips when it's not convenient to carry the additional weight of bottled water or when not enough water can be carried for the duration of the trip.

Giardiasis is something you don't want to get. It can cause many disagreeable symptoms like acute abdominal pain, severe intestinal gas and bloating, as well as recurrent diarrhea and vomiting, that can last up to three to four weeks. Without immediate medical attention, people can end up in the hospital. According to the vet, dogs can get Giardiasis and other ailments from drinking contaminated water. If a dog becomes infected, symptoms will include diarrhea and vomiting. Contact your vet immediately to obtain treatment. For the day-hikes listed in this book, the author recommends carrying all water.

GET INTO CONDITION AND KEEP FIT!

Dogs (and people) should be in fairly good physical condition before embarking on any of the hikes in this book. A dog can be just as out-of-shape as a person. Both need to build strength and endurance for hiking. It is really hard to carry an exhausted fifty pound dog five miles back to the car.

Start by trying a few of the easy hikes listed in this book, then move on to the more difficult ones. There are more easier hikes in the Santa Monica Mountains than in the San Gabriels. Any trip can be a challenge if you or your dog are not in shape. The author recommends the Sulphur Springs Trail in Cheeseboro Canyon as a first time hike. It's a well-traveled, essentially flat trail which gently rambles through magnificent groves of oak and sycamore trees.

The key to training is to start off flat and easy, eventually adding mileage and hills to build endurance and to do it regularly. Syd started off on this regimen:

First week: Easy walks 3 times a week minimum. Around the block is fine.

Second week: Continue the easy walks. Add one long walk with ups and downs increasing mileage to 1-2 miles or increase the number of short walks.

Third week: Continue daily walks. Add one moderate hike with hills, about 400-800 feet of gain with more mileage, and carry 2 liters of water in a daypack on your back. Carrying a daypack is a great way to build strength. Do this once a week plus the flat walks.

Fourth week: Note your progress. Are you and your dog ready for more difficult hikes? Monitor your progress and keep on walking!

WHAT ABOUT MY OLD DOG?

During my seminars on dog hiking someone will always ask, "What about my old dog?" An old hiking dog may never lose the desire to want to go with you. Though he may not be able to keep up on the trails any longer, customize an easy walk for just your older dog, as far as the backyard. Leave the younger dogs at home so the old dog can go at his own speed. I take my oldest dog out on a short little walk to the grassy part of the backyard, letting her sniff and sit at her own pace. She gets so far and lays down. I pull up a chair and spend time with her, giving her my special attention.

FIRST AID

Many items in a first aid kit for people work on a dog. A roll of one inch waterproof tape, some 2.25" x 3" medium adhesive pads and one or two rolls of gauze come in handy for taping sensitive paw pads or barbed wire accidents. An anti-bacterial ointment like neosporine can be used to disinfect scrapes and cuts. Tweezers can be used to remove ticks or cactus spines; needle nose pliers for removing stubborn cholla and cactus spines if hiking in the desert. If your dog wears hiking boots to protect his paws, carry a spare set just in case one is lost or torn.

EVACUATING YOUR DOG

A word here about evacuating your dog. We've not yet had to carry one of our dogs out of the backcountry, but we have watched other people do it. One friend carried her dog on her shoulders, wrapped around her neck like a scarf. Others have loaded a dog in their pack, which is fine, if the dog is small enough to fit. If your dog gets sore paws, is injured, or becomes too tired to walk back to the car, be prepared to handle the situation. It's just something to know about. If you and your dog are in good condition, the chances of this happening will be greatly reduced.

WILDERNESS SANITATION

A large unsightly pile in the middle of the trail should be reason enough to want to dispose of the gifts your dog leaves behind, however there is a better reason: human and canine feces contaminate precious water sources.

There are many products for scooping waste: plastic baggy gloves, scoopers, zip-locks bags. Start collecting those plastic grocery and produce section bags. On the trail, far from trash cans, I loop a carabiner through a knot tied on a plastic bag and clip the bag to the outside of my daypack.

POISON OAK

Poison oak grows with a vengeance in Southern California, especially in the canyons of the Santa Monicas, the Hollywood Hills, the Verdugos and Griffith Park from spring through the end of fall. Don't touch it! If you are allergic to poison oak, a red bumpy rash will appear a few days after initial contact. Depending on the severity of the reaction, calamine lotion or over-the-counter hydrocortisone cream can relieve the itching. Severe outbreaks require a visit to the doctor. We know of one fellow who was dayhiking in the San Bernardino Mountains when he realized the ridge he walked down was covered with poison oak. He jumped into a nearby stream and scrubbed head to toe. Either he wasn't allergic to the pesky flora or the washing worked. He never had a reaction.

Dogs can be allergic to anything and poison oak is no exception. Canine allergy symptoms include the chewing of paws, scratching, and pawing at ears. People can get poison oak by touching animal fur that has been in contact with poison oak. If you have questions about poison oak, contact your physician or veterinarian.

HEAT EXHAUSTION

Heat exhaustion is a problem every summer on sunny Southern California trails especially in the Santa Monica Mountains. The best way to avoid heat injury is to hike early in the morning before 8am or in the evening. There are a number of factors that can cause heat exhaustion in people and dogs: not drinking enough water (dehydration) and physical overexertion when it's too hot.

Human symptoms of heat exhaustion include physical weakness, dizziness, nausea, vomiting and headache. If a hiking partner displays any of these symptoms, have them sit or lie down, preferably with feet elevated, out of direct sunlight. They must rest and drink water with electrolyte additive like Gatorade or Gookinaid until they are hydrated. Cool the skin down by patting the face and head with water.

CANINE SYMPTOMS include vomiting (especially after drinking), a stumbling gait, overall exhaustion, glassy or tired-looking eyes. Heat combined with dehydration and overexertion will have detrimental effects on a dog. Get the dog into shade and pat water on his head,

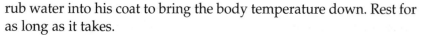

rub water into his coat to bring the body temperature down. Rest for as long as it takes.

When we first began hiking with our dogs in the San Gabriel Mountains, Syd was really out of shape. Along the trail, she ran for shade and started vomiting. By the time we got back to the car, she was completely exhausted, barely able to move: the result of heat, overexertion, dehydration and quite possibly a touch of altitude sickness. We opted for easier walks until she was in better condition, carried more water, stopped more often for water breaks and rubbed water on her head and along her back.

We sweat while dogs cool themselves by breathing, panting. A dog with a long snout can ventilate better than a dog with a short snout. Heat is especially dangerous for short-snouted dogs like pugs and boxers, older dogs, and dogs with heavy fur coats are more prone to the negative effects of heat.

HYPOTHERMIA

Hypothermia is caused by exposure to cold and moisture. Ignoring its symptoms can cause death. As we experience heat loss, our body's core temperature drops, impairing brain and muscular functions.

Hypothermia's initial symptoms include chills and shivering followed by numbness of the skin, muscular impairment, slow hand movement and increased difficulty talking. As the body temperature drops, the muscles become increasingly uncoordinated, there is a slowness of pace, mild confusion, apathy and amnesia. In severe cases, inability to walk or stand, confusion, dilation of pupils, unconsciousness and eventually death. To save a life, restore the body temperature with warm, dry clothes, quick energy food, and a "human sandwich"–wrap your warm body around the person.

Preventing hypothermia requires layered clothing, food, and water. Drink a liquid with an electrolyte additive like Gatorade or Gookinaid to avoid dehydration. Eat snacks high in carbohydrates at frequent intervals to provide and restore energy for physical activity and production of body heat.

CANINE SYMPTOMS include uncontrollable shivering, weakness, difficulty moving, and a stumbling gait.

k.d. once broke through a snowbank, fell into Rock Creek in the Sierra Nevada, and was soaked to the bone. A winter storm was coming in fast, dark gray clouds overhead and a cold wind blowing. By the time we got to the car, she was shivering uncontrollably. I wrapped her in a towel and turned the car heater on full blast, but she was still shivering. My husband got into the back of the car and held her, rubbing her down to warm her. With the warmth of a human body next to her and two big dog biscuits later, she finally stopped shivering.

DRESS IN LAYERS

Cotton shorts and tee-shirts are great for summer hiking. When cotton gets wet it takes forever to dry, holding in cold and moisture. In the San Gabriel Mountains, I always carry a nylon rain jacket, rain pants, a lightweight polypro top and long underwear in my daypack just in case my comfortable cotton t-shirt gets wet or the weather changes. Synthetic materials like polypro and pile are the best insulators against cold and moisture, are lighter weight than wool, dry quickly if they get wet while retaining their insulating properties.

Dressing in layers allows adjustment to outdoor temperature changes: polypropylene top and bottom; synthetic sweater; waterproof, breathable nylon rain jacket that doubles as a windbreaker; a hat, one for sun, one in the pack for warmth; polypro gloves.

NATIVE SPECIES

Development in Los Angeles and Southern California–residential, commercial, industrial–continues to rapidly encroach upon the dwindling habitats of California native wildlife: mountain lions, black bear, deer, coyote, red-tailed hawks and golden eagles.

Freeways and neighborhoods have created land islands that have trapped native species forever. Some islands are bigger than others. On the smaller islands, like Griffith Park and the Verdugo Hills, the largest natives to survive are the coyotes. Along Portuguese Bend, the coyotes are long gone.

New developments in Riverside, San Bernardino and San Diego Counties have locked in precious water sources with four lane roads.

Coyotes and other natives are killed just trying to cross roads to get a drink of water. Fires exacerbate the problem wiping out protective chaparral, exposing habitat to predators. A terrible example of this is in Lake Elsinore, where on east Railroad Canyon Road thousands of new houses are being built. Between the native chaparral and the strip of land that preserves one precious canyon stream is a four lane road that wildlife must cross to get a drink of water. At least one coyote is killed each day on the road trying to get to the water. Especially sad, was the death of a coyote following a fire in the open space. My husband said to me, "Imagine the trauma the coyote experienced *and survived* with the fire, only to be killed by a speeding motorist trying to get to work on time."

Encounters between people and native species, especially the visible ones–coyotes, bears and mountain lions–will continue to occur. Give them respect. Be tolerant. Understand.

A LEASH FOR WILDLIFE PRESERVATION

With human intrusion come domestic dogs. Benefiting from their close association with people and their genetic ties to wolves, domestic dogs unwittingly interfere with the habitat of native species by marking territory, sniffing burrows, chasing lizards and other animals. We can do our small part to help protect threatened native wildlife populations in Southern California by keeping our dogs leashed with us on and off the trails.

RATTLESNAKES

Rattlesnakes and ticks are a part of the natural environment of our western mountain ranges, and are about the best reason I can think of to keep my dogs clipped to my belt loop. Watch for rattlesnakes in the spring, summer and early fall especially in the Santa Monica Mountains and Griffith Park. A rattlesnake bite can kill a dog and access to medical attention must be immediate. AVOIDANCE is the key. There are classes on how to avoid rattlesnakes, but using my hands-free leashing method is the best defense!

TICK CHECK

I carry a DEET-free insect repellent called Natrapel for humans which I rub on my dogs to minimize bites from ticks (Lyme disease) and mosquitos (West Nile Virus). It works.

After every hike, give your dogs a full-body tick check. Run your hands through the fur, from the head to the end of tail. Ticks feel like small, protruding moles and measure from an 1/8" to 1/2" depending on how long they have been attached.

REMOVING A TICK: Use a pair of tweezers to pull it out. Push the dog's hair away from the affected area. Place the tweezers closest to the point of tick contact with the dog, nearest to the tick's head (which is beneath the skin). Get a good firm grasp of the tick with the tweezers and pull it out with firm, dedicated force. Remove any leftover tick parts with the tweezers and clean the affected area with soap and water or rubbing alcohol. Contact your vet with any questions. On the trail, we carry prepackaged alcohol pads to disinfect both human and canine wounds.

Check yourself for ticks especially if they've been hiking in terrain with brush and tall grass. It is horrifying to find the little blood suckers in warm moist places! Case in point: I hiked with a friend to the top of Pilot Knob in the Southern Sierra. We both wore shorts. Only I put on an insect repellent with DEET. By the time we got back to the car, his rear-end was covered with ticks. I had not a one on me!

MOSQUITOES

Mosquitoes bite dogs and are a terrible nuisance, though not as much on dry Southern California trails. In the Sierra Nevada, they have swarmed my dogs and made them cry. To repel insects, use a DEET-free insect repellent. I rub it on my hands then spread it over my dogs' fur, head to tail, careful not to get it in their eyes.

MOUNTAIN LIONS AND BEARS

In all the years we have hiked the local mountains, we have never seen a bear, though we have seen plenty of shotgun-toting hunters. Once, we saw two mountain lions, impressive, beautiful animals, each sighted in coastal mountain ranges: one above Leo Carillo State Beach (dogs not permitted) and the other in Cuyamaca State Park in San Diego County, about thirty feet from our car.

Though your chance of being struck by lightning is greater than that of being attacked by a mountain lion and of winning the California Lottery, there are a few things to know! Mountain lions are nocturnal, hunting primarily at night. They hunt mule deer, but also survive on a diet of small mammals. Attacks are quick and usually come without warning: they stalk and ambush their prey from behind. **LIVING WITH CALIFORNIA MOUNTAINS LIONS:** The California Department of Fish and Game publishes a FREE pamphlet called *Living with California Mountain Lions*, available at most Angeles National Forest ranger stations or directly from Fish & Game by mail request at 1416 Ninth Street, Sacramento, CA 95814; Phone: (916) 445-0411, FAX: (916) 653-1856. The pamphlet offers excellent advice about how to avoid mountain lion encounters and what to do if you should have one.

Hike with a friend, a group, or your dog. Two moving objects are more intimidating than one. Studies have shown that mountain lions are especially attracted to children so keep small kids close to you. Never approach a lion. If you inadvertently meet up with one, give it a way to escape. Running from a mountain lion stimulates their instinct to chase. Try not to crouch or bend over (a person bending over or squatting looks like four-legged prey to a lion). Do all you can to appear larger; remain standing, raise your arms and wave them slowly while speaking in a firm, loud voice; throw stones, branches, whatever you get in your hands without turning your back or bending over. Fight back if attacked, remain standing and face the lion. People have fought them off successfully using rocks, sticks, garden tools, jackets and their bare hands.

Bear sightings are more rare in the local mountains, though encounters with bears have become increasingly common in the Sierra Nevada, primarily due to improper food storage by humans. Currently, bear canisters (black plastic containers used to store food on overnight trips) are required on many Sierra Nevada trails, but are not a concern in our local mountains.

When traveling in any wilderness environment know where your dog is at all times. Park rangers stress the value of keeping your dog on a leash when hiking. Hands-free leashing can save a dog's life when unexpected situations arise on the trail.

PACK YOUR DAYPACK

Daypacks come in varyious sizes for people and dogs and are great for loading everything needed for an enjoyable day: food, water, first aid. On day hikes, I carry all of the water for my dogs and myself. Depending on the hike, that translates into four liters of water. Two-liter plastic soda bottles are an inexpensive and lightweight water bottle solution. First aid items include a pair of tweezers (for removing ticks, splinters or spines), moleskin or waterproof tape and gauze (for protecting against or patching blisters or cut paws) and an antibacterial ointment like neosporine and the items listed below.

People:
1. Map
2. Compass
3. Flashlight, spare batteries
4. Food and water
5. Clothing (lightweight rain jacket/pants that can also double as a windbreaker; wool or synthetic sweater)
6. Pocket knife
7. Matches in waterproof container
8. Hat, sun glasses, sunscreen
9. Cell phone (reception on high points but not in most canyons)
10. First aid kit (tweezers, neosporine, bandages, waterproof tape)

Dogs:
1. Water
2. Bowl
3. ID tag
4. Leash
5. Zip-lock with snacks and/or dry dog food

In the car:
1. One-gallon jug of spare water minimum
2. Bowl
3. Paper towels and plastic bags (for car sickness or other accidents)

COMFORTABLE SHOES

A pair of comfortable hiking boots with good soles is essential. Walking for miles on blistered heels is a miserable experience. Dog paws are also sensitive to rough terrain. Sore, cut, or worn-out paw pads are probably the most common reasons for having to carry a dog out of the backcountry. Making a set of dog boots using the pattern provided in this book is a good way to avoid this problem. You can try dog packs on dayhikes. Dogs have more fun without them. Padded dog packs are better for overnight trips where a couple of days will make a difference in the amount of weight carried.

DOG HIKING BOOTS

The best canine hiking boots are made from soft, pliable leather or suede. Following years of experimentation fellow K9 hiker, Terry Austin, discovered that he could make boots with relative ease for his Golden Retriever, Tama. Using suede, shoelaces and two simple

BARBEE GIVES SADIE A LIFT
PHOTO: PETE YAMAGATA

tools, the boots Terry designed for Tama were a very practical solution for protecting his paws on rugged terrain or on long hikes.

Using the basic pattern shown on the following pages (final size will vary depending on the size of your dog's paws), a set of four suede booties with spares, can be easily made for a reasonable cost. When you are ready to make the boots, first size your dog's paws with a sample boot pattern cut from paper or cloth. This way, you should be able to get an exact fit without expending any of your real materials. Nylon shoelaces are durable and seem to be the best material for longevity. They must be tied fairly tight around the paws so the boots do not slip or fall off.

TAMA MODELS HIS BOOTS

HOW TO MAKE YOUR OWN DOG HIKING BOOTS

Materials needed: good quality suede leather, a hole-punching tool, an eye-riveting tool and 27" nylon shoelaces.

Using the pattern on the next two pages, cut samples out of paper or fabric to determine sizing for all four paws. Trace the pattern onto leather using a light color pencil. Cut the boot shape out of the leather. Punch holes for laces, front claws. Rivet holes for laces only. Lace shoelaces (use different colors for a stylish look) through holes, and presto! A new set of fine hiking boots for your canine companion!

TERRY PUTS ON SLEEPY TAMA'S BOOTS DURING A TRAIL BREAK

TERRY AUSTIN'S PATTERN FOR DOG HIKING BOOTS

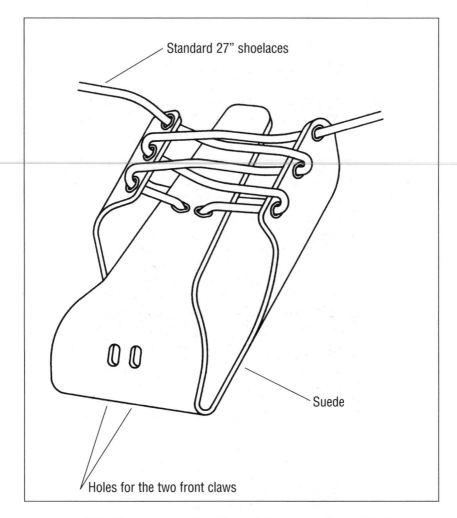

Standard 27" shoelaces

Suede

Holes for the two front claws

Materials needed: good quality suede leather, a hole-punching tool,
an eye-riveting tool and 27" nylon shoelaces.

Dimensions shown on these pages are for larger dogs.
Customize lengths and widths to fit your dog's paws.
Drawings shown are not to size.

CANINE BOOT DESIGN AND DRAWINGS BY TERRY AUSTIN ©1995-2004

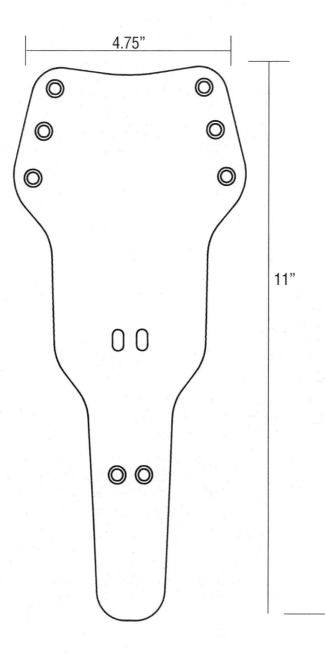

HIKING WITH A GROUP

If you are thinking about hiking with your dog for the first time, consider hiking with a group. There are many in the Los Angeles area that sponsor dog hikes. The Sierra Club's Angeles Chapter is by far the largest and sponsors many FREE, canine-friendly day hikes, evening hikes and weekend trips. At least once a week, a Sierra Club groups leads a free two-hour evening hike with dogs to the top of Mt. Hollywood in Griffith Park. Another sponsors a K9 conditioning hike in San Pedro. One of the first organized canine hiking groups of its kind in the country, the Angeles Chapter's K9 Committee conducts many hikes in Los Angeles. Call the Angeles Chapter at (213) 387-4287 or pick up a copy of the Angeles Chapter's Schedule of Activities, available at Sports Chalet and REI. Their website is: www.angeles.sierraclub.org

MAPS

Directions to trailheads, driving instructions and maps for each hike in this book are listed at the top of each hike description. For most of the drives listed in the book, an Automobile Club of Southern California Los Angeles and Vicinity map or an up-to-date Thomas Guide will work.

Topographic maps (topos) are surveyed and drawn by the United States Geographical Survey, the USGS. In the not so distant past, one could readily buy USGS 15-minute (minute refers to latitude and longitude) maps that displayed a much larger area, but have been phased out in favor of the more detailed 7.5-minute maps or quadrangles (quads) that show half the area of the old maps. Most topos are available at local outdoor equipment supply or travel stores. Older topos show only the geographical details not the trails, since most of the trails were constructed after the areas were surveyed and the maps printed.

The *Trail Maps of the Santa Monica Mountains* series is highly recommended and can be purchased from REI, Sports Chalet and the Santa Monica Mountains National Recreation Area park headquarters at 30401 Agoura Road, Suite 100 in Agoura Hills. FREE National Park Service maps are also available for some of the more popular recreation areas in the Santa Monica Mountains.

TRAIL ACCESS

Every government agency, city, county, state or federal, that oversees public park lands, has its own set of rules concerning dogs, including but not limited to the use of leashes, owner control and access. Regulations are usually posted at the trailhead or indicated on the wilderness permit if one is needed.

There is nothing more frustrating then getting up at o'dark-thirty

RUSKIE CONTEMPLATES THE NO PETS SIGN PHOTO: JULIE RUSH

to pack for a full-day's excursion into the backcountry with your dog, drive an hour or more to a trailhead, only to discover a big posted sign declaring that dogs are not allowed on the trails.

One time, we drove almost three hours to hike with our dogs to the top of Suicide Rock in the San Jacinto Mountains near Palm Springs. We picked up our permit at the USFS office and were told that dogs were allowed on the trails. It was even written on the permit. We parked at the signless trailhead and started the hike. About a quarter mile up the trail, we were greeted by a big sign stating "no dogs on trails." Why? We crossed from USFS lands and had entered a California State Park where dogs were not permitted. Just a mile or two up the same trail, where it crossed back into national forest, dogs were allowed. It pays to call ahead if you're unsure about the regulations concerning dogs. In an area where dogs are permitted off leash, they must be trained to respond immediately to voice commands.

All owners are responsible for their dog's behavior on the trail and for knowing all the rules that apply to dogs for the particular area they'll be visiting.

BRING YOUR ADVENTURE PASS TO THE SAN GABRIELS

A National Forest Adventure Pass must be displayed on all vehicles parked in the Angeles Forest. The pass is required in the Angeles,

Los Padres, San Bernardino, and Cleveland National Forests. Cars without the pass will be ticketed. Adventure Passes can be purchased from the USFS and other retailers, must be displayed on your parked vehicle on any visit to the Angeles National Forest.

Throughout southern California there are a large number of places where dogs are not allowed, leashed or unleashed outside of parking lots or campgrounds: beaches, most national parks, monuments, and historic sites, state parks and wilderness. Dogs are allowed with few regulations on land managed by the Bureau of Land Management (BLM), the United States Forest Service (USFS), local jurisdictions (cities and counties) and most national recreation areas supervised by the Santa Monica Mountains National Recreation Area. Leash requirements are usually posted at the park entrance or on backcountry use permits. If you have any questions, call the supervising land agency before your trip.

DOGS AND BEACHES

Salty ocean water and beach sand imbeds in dog fur making the skin itch and is hard to wash out. Precious marine life found in tide pools already combats coastal pollution, natural predators and people. Beaches are shadeless. For many reasons, dogs are currently prohibited from all state beaches in Los Angeles County with the exception of the Long Beach Dog Zone, a 2-3 acre area on Ocean Avenue in Belmont Shores between Argonne and Roycroft (a temporary pilot program–check ahead to make sure it is open) and some small stretches of rugged virtually inaccessible beaches along the Palos Verdes Estates Shoreline Preserve.

MINI BOSTONS BEANIE AND BOOBOO
POSE FOR THEIR DAD

RATING THE HIKES FOR DIFFICULTY

With the exception of some slippery steep scrambling on the hike to the Dominator, technical skill for dog or owner is not necessary on the hikes in this book. A healthy set of lungs and the desire to have a wonderful time are all that's required. Ratings of diffiuclty are based on mileage, elevation gain and dog abilities and are as follows:

EASY: Good hikes for dogs and people just starting out on the trail, older dogs, small dogs, out-of-shape dogs and people looking for some weekend exercise, or who are getting into shape for more challenging trips.

MODERATE: Dogs and people should be in good physical condition, should be walking two to three times a week, a total of 2-4 miles.

STRENUOUS: Dogs and people should be experienced hikers, in excellent physical condition with a weekly exercise routine that includes 4-6 miles per week with hill climbing (or ups and downs).

The hikes in this book have been walked, timed and rated by my dogs: k.d., a slender, long-legged forty pound Doberman/Whippet mix; Syd, a plump, 65-pound short-legged Australian cattle dog; Ruby, a 45-pound cattle dog; and KoKo, a small Chow-cattle dog mix. The more you hike with your dog, the easier it will be to judge her hiking ability, skill level and water needs (two liters minimum *just for your dog*). Listed in the hike headings are the minimum water requirements for a medium-sized dog, based on moderate (spring or early fall) Southern California temperatures.

Carry a spare gallon of water and a bowl in your car.
Many of the trailheads for the hikes listed in this book are dry!
Water is the most important item you can carry.

CALABASAS BARK PARK BELOW A TRAIL IN THE SANTA MONICA MOUNTAINS NATIONAL RECREATION AREA

THE SANTA MONICA MOUNTAINS

The Santa Monica Mountains are the perfect training ground for dogs and owners training for the more demanding terrain of the San Gabriel Mountains. From Griffith Park in the east; Point Mugu to the west; the Pacific Ocean to the south; the San Fernando and Conejo Valleys to the north, this coastal range is rich in history. Prehistoric habitation dates back thousands of years to the ancestors of the Chumash, Fernandino and Gabrieleno people. Spanish explorers and missionaries followed later. By the end of the 19th century, pioneer families built and worked their farms and ranches in the Santa Monica Mountains.

The plant communities of the Santa Monica Mountains are varied, from coastal marsh along the ocean's tidewater zone, to the coastal sage scrub and chaparral of the open rolling ridges, to the oak and riparian woodlands found in canyons and streambeds. Native species include a small population of mountain lions, mule deer, coyotes, rodents, and a variety of lizards, birds and snakes. Now and then, in the early evenings before sunset on Cheeseboro Canyon Trails, you can still hear the lonesome yip of a coyote.

The Simi Hills, Palo Comado and Cheeseboro Canyons are to the east of the Santa Monica Mountains. Their unique features include rugged sandstone cliffs, deep canyons, meandering streams, groves of sycamores and wide, open ridges, covered with oaks, grasses and an array of flora. The high point of the Simi Hills is Simi Peak (2,403'), which has nice views from the summit. It is a full day's hike from Cheeseboro Canyon via Palo Comado Canyon.

WATER AND SUN

The Santa Monica Mountains and Simi Hills are HOT during the summer months. Plan hikes in early morning or on a cool evening, *not in the heat of midday!* Carry plenty of water. Autumn, winter and spring are best for hiking the more demanding trails though daytime temperatures can easily climb over eighty degrees any time of the year. And, there is no shade on many of the trails.

ON THE TRAIL TO SANDSTONE PEAK AFTER THE FIRESTORM OF 1993

FIRE

Over the years, devastating fires, unfortunately, mostly man-made, have swept across the Santa Monica Mountains killing people and wildlife, destroying homes and vegetation. It takes several years for the land to recover from these fires.

During periods of great fire hazard, the Santa Monica Mountains National Recreation Area will post fire closures.

SMMNRA PARK HEADQUARTERS AND MAPS

The Santa Monica Mountains National Recreation Area Park Headquarters is located at 30401 Agoura Road, Suite 100 in Agoura Hills, just off the 101-Ventura Freeway. (818) 597-9192. National Park Service maps are also available for some of the more popular recreation areas in the Santa Monica Mountains.

Cartographer Tom Harrison's series "Trail Maps of the Santa Monica Mountains" are highly recommended and can be purchased from sports retailers like REI and Sports Chalet.

CHEESEBORO AND PALO COMADO CANYONS

Cheeseboro Canyon became part of the Santa Monica Mountains National Recreation Area in the late 1980s, under the jurisdiction of the National Park Service. The 2,308 acres of the old Jordan Ranch, which was purchased from comedian Bob Hope and added to the recreation area in 1994, includes beautiful Palo Comado, the large canyon to the west of Cheeseboro. To date, the purchase of Jordan Ranch represents the largest land acquisition in the Santa Monica Mountains National Recreation Area. A walk through Cheeseboro and Palo Comado is a walk back to the past. It land was never developed, with the exception of a few jeep trails and corrals. The small arroyos or mini-canyons in the meadows are a result of grazing erosion. When cattle eat the grass, the ground is exposed to the elements. Ruts become gullies. Gullies become rain-carved canyons.

Cheeseboro Canyon has an extensive network of trails, ranging in difficulty from easy to strenuous. Palo Comado can be accessed on foot, by mountain bike or horse from the parking area at Cheeseboro Canyon though additional entrances to the canyon have been planned for many years. As of this writing the official entrance is still at Cheeseboro Canyon. Few foot trails exist within the newly dedicated Palo Comado Canyon area. Most are old jeep trails. One spur trail, we called the "Bone Yard" led to a pit where the old ranchers buried dead cattle. The coyotes dug up and scattered the carcasses, leaving just the bones, many bones that bleached white in the sun.

The Park Service is always working on acquiring additional funding to provide trailside amenities like picnic tables and restrooms and to maintain trails. On one of our scouting trips to Palo Comado several years ago, we ran into two rangers on horseback who were in the process of exploring what appeared to be trails once used by the ranchers to herd sheep between Cheeseboro and Palo Comado. Palo Comado is truly an exceptional addition to the Santa Monica Mountains National Recreation Area. It is a wonderful place to explore and leashed dogs are welcome on all of the trails in both canyon areas.

We first walked the trails of Cheeseboro Canyon on a late spring weekend several years ago, before it was officially added to the national park system. The dirt parking lot was empty; there were no other people on the trails, just the sounds of crickets, the grasses rustling in the wind and the occasional cry of hawks circling in the sky.

That experience contrasted sharply with more recent trips to Cheeseboro Canyon following its addition to the park system. Though protected from urban development, the park is a very popular place on the weekends. The once quiet gem of the Santa Monica Mountains is now frequented by mountain bikers, equestrians, hikers, families and groups. Most of the visitors seem to stick to lower canyon trails, so it is still possible to enjoy the tranquillity of the higher ridge trails, like the Baleen Wall Trail.

For the past 150 years, ranchers have grazed cattle in these hills and the effect of grazing on the land can be seen by the trained eye. Small arroyos primarily created by over-grazing, are a land formation that did not exist prior to the introduction of cattle in the west and are evident in Palo Comado Canyon. Many of the native species of plants have been replaced by non-natives.

However, both canyons are still home to Coast Live Oak , Valley Oak, California Black Walnut, willow, lupine and Fuchsia-flowered Gooseberry. Non-native species like the exotic tree tobacco which is a native of South America, can be found in the uppermost regions of Palo Comado Canyon. An interesting note about the name Palo Comado: in Spanish, Palo means "thin trees" or "poles," yet there is no exact translation for Comado. There has been some speculation that at one time the canyon was called "Palo Quemado" meaning "burned trees" in Spanish.

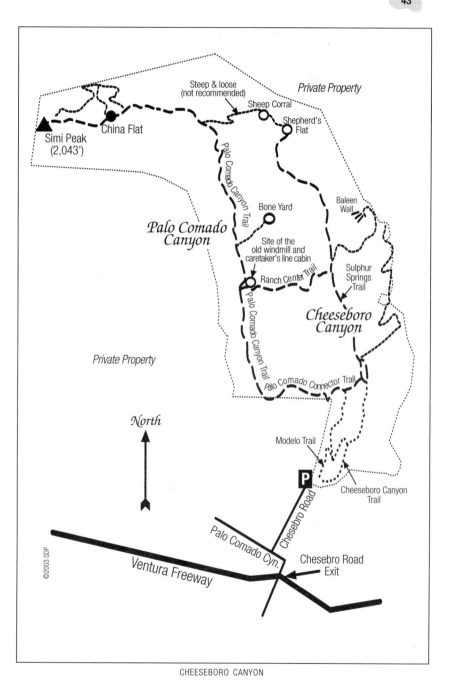

CHEESEBORO CANYON

HIKING IN CHEESEBORO AND PALO COMADO CANYONS

Rating: Easy to strenuous as noted
Recommended for: Varies by hike
Mileage: Varies by hike
K9 water: Varies by hike, recommend 2 quarts minimum, seasonal stream
Posted: Pets on leash. Recommend cleaning up after your pet
Ambience: Rolling grasslands, shaded canyons, oaks and raptors
Maps: Automobile Club of Southern California Los Angeles and Vicinity
Hiking maps: USGS Calabasas and Thousand Oaks 7.5 minute topos (1967 map does not show all trails)
Best time to hike: Upper ridge trails, November to April. Canyon trails all year. Carry water at all times. Plan hikes for early morning and on cool evenings.

DRIVING

From the 101-Ventura Freeway, exit at Chesebro Road (note difference in spelling). Turn right on Palo Comado Road toward old Agoura Hills. Pass under "Old Agoura" sign and turn right at first stop sign, Chesebro Road.

Drive approximately 0.7 miles to the Cheeseboro Canyon Park entrance on the right (0.2 miles past a one lane bridge). Turn right into the park entrance and drive another 0.2 miles to a dirt parking area. There is a portable restroom in the parking area.

NOTE

All hikes for Cheeseboro/Palo Comado listed in this book start at the Cheeseboro parking lot described in the driving directions at the beginning of this section. As of this writing, the gate to the main parking lot opens at 8am and closes at sunset. If you think your hike might take you past sunset or you want to start a little earlier, park outside the entrance and walk in to the park.

BALEEN WALL VIA CHEESEBORO CANYON

Rating: Strenuous
Recommended for: Well-conditioned dogs
Mileage: 900' of gain, 7 miles, 3-4 hours round-trip on fire road
K9 water: 2 quarts minimum
Posted: Pets on leash. Recommend cleaning up after your pet
Ambience: Shaded canyons, rolling grasslands away from the crowds
Best time to hike: November to April. Get an early morning start.

HIKING

From the parking lot at Cheeseboro Canyon, walk straight ahead on the main dirt road, passing an informational sign. Paralleling the dirt road is a seasonal stream which meanders through the canyon, providing water to a variety of wildlife within the park. Once past the Overlook Trail sign on the right, the terrain opens up, grasslands, rounded open ridges and scattered oaks. About a half-hour to forty-five minute walk from the parking lot, reach the Sulfur Springs/Baleen Wall Trails fork. Go right on the Baleen Wall Trail.

Follow the Baleen Wall Trail as it climbs out of the main canyon, up onto open ridges. The trail winds its way through the hills, passing a signed service road, a big water tank and some power lines. When the jagged, gray, teethy-looking Baleen Wall is in view and about 1/4 mile walk away (named after the Baleen Whale's teeth) notice a fork. The road to the right can be followed to the cliffs, where one can have a nice picnic lunch. To descend back into Cheeseboro Canyon, turn left at the same fork. The trail appears to head toward a lone powerline. About 200' past the fork, turn right onto a narrow foot path that quickly descends into Cheeseboro Canyon, but provides a nice view of the Baleen Wall on the way down. At the bottom of the canyon, turn left (west) and follow the trail through the canyon back to the parking lot.

TIRED BABY   PHOTO: JULIE RUSH

SIMI PEAK (2,403') VIA PALO COMADO CANYON

Rating: Very strenuous!
Recommended for: Well-conditioned dogs only!!
Mileage: 2,000' of gain, 16 miles, 6-7 hours round-trip on fire road
K9 water: 2 quarts minimum, no water on route
Posted: Pets on leash. Recommend cleaning up after your pet
Ambience: Long gradual ascent to the top of Simi Peak
Best time to hike: During moderate weather, late fall through spring, October through April
There is little or no shade on most of the open ridges and uphill segments of the hike. A few stands of oak are scattered along the open ridges, but the canyons are well-shaded by old, stately oaks.

HIKING

From the parking lot at Cheeseboro Canyon park entrance follow the trail marked "Modelo Trail" on the left side of the parking lot. Walk the trail as it climbs an open ridge with a narrow canyon on the right. At the top of the ridge, turn left at the fork, continuing on the signed "Modelo Trail." The trail continues along the ridge top with Cheeseboro Canyon to the right. Follow the trail over a slight rise and down the other side to a second fork. Turn left at the second fork (the fork on the right returns to Cheeseboro Canyon and makes a nice easy, 3 mile loop). Follow the trail as it contours around a ridge, skirting several minor canyons. The trail finally begins its descent into Palo Comado Canyon. The stables of a pony club come into view at the canyon bottom. The trail passes to the right of the stables, and meanders through beautiful Palo Comado Canyon. When we scouted this hike, we saw a herd of five mule deer just past the stables, while hawks and turkey buzzards flew in the sky above.

A little over a mile from the stables, you'll pass by some Southern California Gas pipeline signs and come to a third, main trail fork. This was the site of the last caretaker's dwelling (a dilapidated silver trailer) for the old Jordan Ranch. When the first edition of this book came out, the trailer and an old windmill were still standing at the fork and were used as landmarks. Both have since been removed. The fork to the right, the Ranch Center Trail, returns to Cheeseboro Canyon and is the return route for this hike. Continue north on the trail straight ahead to the left.

MOUNTAIN BIKERS APPROACHING THE OLD CORRAL AT CHINA FLATS

Follow the trail, as it leaves the canyon and begins a gradual, but steep ascent uphill. As the trail climbs steadily, jagged sandstone cliffs come into view. At the base of the first distinct set of cliffs is the old Sheep Corral Trail which was once used by the ranchers to herd sheep to and from neighboring Cheeseboro Canyon. Following the 1994 Northridge Earthquake and subsequent aftershocks, the trail was closed indefinitely due to landslides.

The main trail passes the cliffs and soon enters a vast, beautiful high valley, known as China Flats. Pass an old corral on the right and a road fork. Follow the left fork. A pond, used for watering livestock, comes into view on the left. About 1/4 mile past the corral, turn left at another fork and head towards the valley. At the next fork, stay right (the left fork goes down to Thousand Oaks). There is a small stream and rocky cliffs to the left of the trail. The trail leaves the valley, and comes to a saddle and another fork where Simi Valley comes into view. Continue straight ahead on the left fork. Follow the trail to the summit of Simi Peak. There is a fine view of Sandstone Peak, tallest mountain in the Santa Monicas to the west.

Return by the same route. When you reach the fork where the old caretaker's trailer used to be, turn left on the Ranch Center Trail. The trail climbs a steep ridge, but then quickly descends into Cheeseboro Canyon. At the bottom of the canyon, turn right and follow the trail back through the canyon to the parking lot. Following a good spring rain, the canyon is filled with croaking frogs.

PALO COMADO CANYON TO CHEESEBORO CANYON VIA THE RANCH CENTER TRAIL

Rating: Moderate
Recommended for: Small well-conditioned dogs
Mileage: 1,200' of gain, 7.9 miles, 3-4 hours round-trip on trail and fire road
K9 water: 2 quarts minimum, no water on route
Posted: Pets on leash. Recommend: cleaning up after your pet
Ambience: Wander through canyons and oaks
Best time to hike: October to late April

HIKING

From the parking lot at Cheeseboro Canyon park entrance follow the trail marked "Modelo Trail" on the left side of the parking lot. Walk the trail as it climbs up an open ridge with a narrow canyon on the right. At the top of the ridge, turn left at the fork, continuing on the signed "Modelo Trail." The trail continues along the ridge top with Cheeseboro Canyon to the right. Follow the trail over a slight rise and down the other side to a second fork.

Turn left at the second fork. This is the Palo Comado Connector Trail (a right turn on this trail will take you back to the Sulphur Springs Trail in Cheeseboro Canyon). Follow the left fork, the trail contours around a ridge, skirting several minor canyons. The trail finally begins its descent into Palo Comado Canyon and the stables of a pony club become visible at the bottom. The trail passes to the right of the stables. The trail (which is one of the old ranch jeep trails) meanders through beautiful Palo Comado Canyon. When we scouted this hike, we saw a herd of five mule deer on the open ridges just past the stables. There were also plenty of hawks and turkey buzzards in the sky above.

A little over a mile from the stables, you'll pass by some Southern California Gas pipeline signs and come to a third, main trail fork. Just past the signs, was the old windmill, and the site of the last care-taker's dwelling on the old Jordan Ranch property. When this book was first written, both were still standing. Turn right at this fork (the left fork goes to Simi Peak), now named Ranch Center Trail. In the first edition of this book, we called this "The Old Windmill Hike," since the trail was not yet named, and there was a windmill at the

ONE FOR THE HISTRY BOOKS: THE OLD JORDAN RANCH CARETAKER'S TRAILER HAS BEEN REMOVED. RANCH CENTER TRAIL CONTINUES TO THE RIGHT. THE TRAIL TO SIMI PEAK IS OFF TO THE LEFT.

fork. Follow the trail as it climbs a steep ridge. At the ridge crest, the trail steeply descends into Cheeseboro Canyon. At the bottom of the canyon, turn right and follow the trail back through the canyon to the parking lot.

MODELO TRAIL TO CHEESEBORO CANYON

Rating: Easy
Recommended for: Out-of-shape, older or small dogs
Mileage: 550' of gain, 2.9 miles, 2 hours round-trip on trail and fire road
K9 water: 1 quart minimum, no water on route
Posted: Pets on leash. Recommend: cleaning up after your pet
Ambience: Nice open views of surrounding ridges and Cheeseboro Canyon
Best time to hike: October to late April

HIKING

From the parking lot at Cheeseboro Canyon park entrance follow the trail marked "Modelo Trail" on the left side of the parking lot. Walk the trail as it climbs an open ridge with a narrow canyon on the right. At the top of the ridge, turn left at the fork, continuing on the signed "Modelo Trail." The trail continues along the ridge top with Cheeseboro Canyon to the right.

Follow the trail over a slight rise and down the other side to a second fork. Turn right at this fork, on the Palo Comado Connector Trail and follow the trail as it descends into Cheeseboro Canyon. At the canyon bottom, turn right, on the Sulphur Springs Trail, and follow it through Cheeseboro Canyon, back to the parking lot.

SULPHUR SPRINGS TRAIL VIA CHEESEBORO CANYON

Rating: Easy
Recommended for: Out-of-shape, older or small dogs
Mileage: 200' of gain, 2.6 miles, 1-2 hours round-trip on trail and fire road
K9 water: 2 quarts minimum, no water on route
Posted: Pets on leash. Recommend cleaning up after your pet
Ambience: Wander through canyons and oaks
Best time to hike: All year

HIKING

From the parking lot at Cheeseboro Canyon, walk straight ahead on the main dirt road, passing an information sign. Paralleling the dirt road is a seasonal stream which meanders through the canyon, providing water to a variety of wildlife within the park.

Follow the trail as it winds its way through the riparian habitat of the canyon. Once past the Overlook Trail sign on the right, the terrain opens up, grasslands, rounded open ridges and scattered oaks. About a half hour, forty-five minute walk from the parking lot, reach a fork and go left on the signed Sulphur Springs Trail. The Baleen Wall Trail is on the right. Before 1997, this trail name was spelled both "Sulfur" and "Sulphur" on many of the same maps. The latter is now used by the Park Service on their new maps. Not far past the signed fork on the Sulphur Springs Trail, is a nice picnic area protected by the umbrella of oak branches and next to the little, rambling stream. Return by the same route.

NOTES

Any hike in Cheeseboro Canyon/Palo Comado can be sweltering during the summer, and very warm on any given day of the year. There is no shade on the high ridge trails and they are not recommended for hiking during the summer (unless done very early in the morning). The shorter hikes through the canyons are preferable during the summer months and suitable for the smallest of dogs. One of the most pleasant hikes in the valley on a warm summer evening is a walk to the picnic area on the Sulphur Springs Trail, about a half hour from the main parking area. Cheeseboro Canyon is home to a diverse group of wildlife including several birds of prey. Golden eagles have been sighted in Palo Comado Canyon and around the Baleen Wall.

ARROYO SEQUIT

Rating: Easy
Recommended for: Out-of-shape, older or small dogs
Mileage: 200' of gain, 0.75 miles, 1 hour round-trip on paved and fire road, over meadow
K9 water: 1 quart minimum, no water on route
Posted: Pets on leash. Recommend cleaning up after your pet
Ambience: A gem in the Santa Monica Mountains, historic ranch site
Maps: Automobile Club of Southern California Los Angeles and Vicinity
Hiking Maps: USGS Triunfo Pass 7.5 minute topo, and Trail Map of the Santa Monica Mountains, Central
Best time to hike: All year. Park gates open from 8am-5pm. Hot during summer.

DRIVING

Exit Kanan Road from the 101-Ventura Freeway and go south on Kanan Rd. At approximately 5.9 miles, turn right on Mulholland Highway. At 1.0 mile, continue right on Mulholland Hwy., at the Encinal Cyn. Rd./Mulholland fork. At 3.2 miles make a left on CA-23 south (Westlake Blvd.). At 1.8 miles, turn right on Mulholland Hwy. Follow Mulholland Hwy. approximately 1.7 miles to the entrance of Arroyo Sequit on the left. Turn left into a small parking area, being careful not to block the gated road.

ALTERNATE DRIVING ROUTE:

Exit Westlake Blvd., from the Ventura Fwy 101 and go south. Follow Westlake Blvd. (Hwy 23 south) 6.9 miles to to Mulholland Highway and turn right. Follow Mulholland approximately 1.7 miles to the entrance of Arroyo Sequit on the left. Turn left into a small parking area, careful not to block the gated road.

HIKING

Walk past locked gate along the paved one-lane road, up a hill. At about 1/8 mile, turn left at a post marked "trail," bypassing the old farmhouse residence on the right. The trail meets the road again, which is now dirt, at a storage barn. There is a portable restroom and a circle of benches, next to the barn. Continue up the dirt road, and pass beneath large, stately oaks (and one or two boisterous frogs) until you reach a large, open hilltop meadow with picnic tables located in various scenic places along the meadow. To the north, you can see the massive, craggy peaks above Pt. Mugu.

EVENING LIGHT AT ARROYO SEQUIT

More adventurous types, can follow the dirt road to its end, just past a powerline. From the meadow, walk the dirt road south, staying right at a fork. The road narrows and drops down into a small canyon where occasionally quail can be sighted. Pass beneath a powerline and the road ends in a few hundred feet. Return by the same route.

NOTES

Arroyo Sequit was once an old pioneer ranch. Enjoy the peace and solitude of this little gem of the Santa Monicas. Arroyo Sequit is a great place to have a picnic or to celebrate a dog's birthday.

PARAMOUNT RANCH HIKES
GENERAL INFORMATION

Rating: Easy to moderate as noted
Recommended for: Out-of-shape, older or small dogs
K9 water: 1-2 quarts, no water on route. Do not drink from Medea Creek
Ambience: Old movie set
Maps: Automobile Club of Southern California Los Angeles and Vicinity
Hiking maps: USGS Point Dume 7.5 minute topo, and Trail Map of the Santa Monica Mountains, Central
Best time to hike: All year. Hot in summer.

DRIVING

Exit Kanan Road from the 101-Ventura Freeway and go south approximately 0.25 mile to signed Cornell Road. Turn left and follow Cornell Road approximately 1.8 miles to the signed park entrance on the right. Follow the main road, staying left, through an open area to a parking area and an information kiosk.

PARAMOUNT RANCH

WALK OF THE TOWN

Rating: Easy
Recommended for: Out-of-shape, older or small dogs
Mileage: 0.5 miles, 0.5 hours round-trip
K9 water: 1 quart, no water on route
Posted: Pets on leash. Recommend cleaning up after your pet
Ambience: Old western movie set
Maps: Automobile Club of Southern California Los Angeles and Vicinity
Best time to hike: All year

HIKING

From the parking area, pass the information kiosk and walk across a
bridge, over Medea Creek, and follow signs to the western town. The
town was used for several years as the setting for many television
series and scores of old westerns. Once, we found a script belonging
to Jane Seymour from the old CBS television series, *Dr. Quinn Medicine
Woman,* on an outlying trail. Walk around the town and then across
the meadow to the old church and graveyard. Bring a blanket, a picnic lunch and sit awhile in the field.

COYOTE CANYON TRAIL

Rating: Easy
Recommended for: Out-of-shape, older or small dogs
Mileage: 100' gain, 0.75 miles, 0.5 hours round-trip
K9 water: 1 quart, no water on route
Posted: Pets on leash. Recommend cleaning up after your pet
Maps: Automobile Club of Southern California Los Angeles and Vicinity
Best time to hike: All year

HIKING

Walk to the west side of town to the signed trail. Follow the narrow dirt
trail as it meanders through a small canyon, paralleling a dry creek to the
left of the trail. At approximately 1/8 mile, go right at a fork (fork is
signed "Overlook Trail" which goes off to the left). The trail passes
through an area of pink volcanic rock, as it contours along a grassy ridge-
line. In another 1/8 mile, there is a picnic table on the left, about 100' off
the trail and hidden in the chaparral. Continue along the trail until it
returns to the paved road behind the town and a large grove of eucalyptus
trees. Turn right and follow the paved road back to town.

MEDEA CREEK TRAIL (AKA STREAM TERRACE TRAIL)

Rating: Easy
Recommended for: Out-of-shape, older or small dogs
Mileage: 300' gain, 1 mile, 0.75 hours round-trip
K9 water: 1 quart, no water on route. Do not drink from Medea Creek.
Posted: Pets on leash. Recommend cleaning up after your pet
Maps: Automobile Club of Southern California Los Angeles and Vicinity
Best time to hike: All year

HIKING

From the information kiosk, walk south across the parking lot past a gated road on the right. On the right, about 100 feet past the gated road is the signed Medea Creek Trail. Follow this narrow use trail as it gradually climbs uphill through thick chaparral and oaks, paralleling the road for about 100 feet or so. Follow the trail as it contours the densely vegetated ridge by a series of short switchbacks, out to an open area and the highway. Turn right at the "5K Trail" fork just before the highway. Continue on the trail to the next fork. If you go right at the fork, you can climb a small hill, via a return loop trail, to a vista point which overlooks the Paramount Ranch and Medea Creek. Return to the main trail, via the loop, and descend gradually back into the canyon. As you descend, the prominent peak across the wash is named Sugarloaf Peak. At the canyon bottom, turn right and follow the dirt road back to the locked gate and parking lot. Medea Creek parallels the dirt road on the left.

OLD RUINS AT ROCKY OAKS

ROCKY OAKS HIKES

Rating: Easy
Recommended for: Out-of-shape, older or small dogs
K9 water: 1 quart, no water on route
Posted: Pets on leash. Recommend cleaning up after your pet
Maps: Automobile Club of Southern California Los Angeles and Vicinity
Hiking Maps: USGS Point Dume 7.5 minute topo, and Trail Map of the Santa Monica Mountains, Central
Best time to hike: All year. These trails, like most in the Santa Monica Mountains, can be very hot during late spring, summer and early fall. Be sure to carry more water at those times. Rocky Oaks is popular with equestrians from neighboring ranches and camps.

DRIVING

Exit Kanan Road from the 101-Ventura Freeway and go south to Mulholland Highway. Turn right on Mulholland and at 0.1 mile turn right again into the park entrance. There is ample parking in the dirt parking lot. Both hikes start from same point near the information kiosk in the parking lot.

ROCKY OAKS LOOP TRAIL

HIKING
Mileage: 200' gain, 1.5 miles, 1 hour round-trip

From the information kiosk at the west end of parking lot (near the entrance) follow the main trail north to a signed trail fork, "Rocky Oaks Loop Trail-Creek Trail." Turn left at the sign and follow the trail as it curves to the right, passing the old ranch ruins and antique farming equipment on the left. At approximately 1/8 mile from the sign, you come to a three-way fork, with the signed "Creek Trail" on the left. Continue straight on the "Loop Trail," heading uphill passing through some wood posts, eventually contouring around a south facing slope (no shade). The trail contours around the ridge passing a small use trail on the left. About twenty-five feet from the main trail on this use trail, there is a sign marking the "Overlook Trail" on the left. For a nice 360-degree view of Rocky Oaks, follow the Overlook Trail to the left, to a small open area about 100' from the Loop Trail. Return to the loop trail by the same route.

GRASSLANDS AT ROCKY OAKS

After returning to the main trail, continue contouring around the ridge toward Kanan Road. At a fork just before the highway (which is separated from the park by a fence), turn right and descend into a canyon of meadows and oaks. At the next fork, the signed "Pond Trail," continue left on the Loop Trail. Go right at the next fork, the signed "Glade Trail," following the trail through a meadow, where crickets can often be heard chirping. At a four-way fork, continue straight ahead, following the sign to the parking lot. Stay left at the next fork and pass through a pleasant shaded picnic area, just before the parking lot. There is a water fountain in the picnic area and restrooms at the parking lot.

ROCKY OAKS CREEK TRAIL

HIKING

Mileage: 50' gain, 1 mile, 0.75 hour round-trip

From the information kiosk at the west end of the parking lot (near the entrance), follow the main trail north to a signed trail fork, Rocky Oaks Loop Trail-Creek Trail. Turn left at the sign and follow the trail as it curves to the right, passing old ranch ruins and antique farming equipment on the left. Approximately 1/8 mile from the sign, you come to a three-way fork, with the signed Creek Trail on left. Turn left and walk across the field to a narrow use trail which parallels a dry creek. Follow the trail about a quarter mile through oaks and scrub, before the park boundary. Return by the same route.

NOTES

The Rocky Oaks area, with its year-round spring, was once home to various bands of coastal Chumash Indians, but any trace of their existence was destroyed by subsequent years of farming and ranching. At the turn of the century, the Thompson family built their ranch above the spring, and raised crops and a few head of cattle. Life was not easy in the Santa Monica Mountains and the family endured the hardships of nature, experiencing fires, floods, windstorms and drought. In 1950, the Brown family built their farm here, naming it Rocky Oaks, raising cattle and crops. In 1980, they sold the property to the National Park Service. The Agoura fire of 1978 destroyed all traces of the Thompson's early pioneer ranch. There is a nice, shaded picnic area located on the east side of the parking lot.

THE BEAUTIFUL OLD RANCH HOUSE AT LAKE ENCHANTO IS NOW A RANGER STATION

PETER STRAUSS RANCH ❧ LAKE ENCHANTO

Once inhabited by the Chumash Indians, traces of their existence have long vanished from this special place nestled in the oaks. In 1923, a fellow named, Harry Miller, built the stone ranch house, caretaker's quarters, aviary and other stone structures on the property.

During the late 1930s, millionaire Charles Hinman purchased the property and constructed a small dam on Triunfo Creek. The lake created by the dam was named Lake Enchanto. In 1939, a swimming pool built just west of the ranch house was the largest swimming pool on the west coast at the time! Around the 1950s, Lake Enchanto became a popular amusement park and children's summer camp. By the 1970s, Hinman lost the property to a tax sale and Lake Enchanto was essentially abandoned. As a kid, I remember driving with my parents by the abandoned, decrepit place on weekend excursions, always wondering what had happened behind the strange stone tower and entrance.

In 1977, actor Peter Strauss purchased the property which was covered with the rusted ruins of Lake Enchanto's abandoned amusement rides. He lived at the ranch house from 1977 to 1983, where he spent hundreds of thousands of dollars on the removal of all the abandoned structures and debris left over from Lake Enchanto days. He made major landscaping and general improvements to the property, then sold the ranch to the Santa Monica Mountains Conservancy. In 1987, the National Park Service purchased it from the Conservancy.

PETER STRAUSS TRAIL

Rating: Easy
Recommended for: Out-of-shape, older or small dogs
Mileage: 200' gain, 0.6 mile, 0.5 hours round-trip
K9 water: 1 quart, no water on route
Posted: Pets on leash, clean up after your pet
Maps: Automobile Club of Southern California Los Angeles and Vicinity
Hiking Maps: USGS Point Dume 7.5 minute topo, and Trail Map of the Santa Monica Mountains, Central
Best time to hike: All year. Late winter and spring are the best times to see wildflowers in bloom. Open daily from 8am to 5pm.

DRIVING

Exit Kanan Road from the 101-Ventura Fwy. and head south approximately 2.8 miles to Troutdale Drive. Turn left and follow Troutdale about 0.4 mile to Mulholland Highway. Turn left at Mulholland, cross over a bridge and turn right into a parking area.

HIKING

From the parking area, follow a foot path back across the bridge and left into the gated Peter Strauss Ranch. Straight ahead is the beautiful old stone ranch house, built in 1923, along with the caretaker's place on the hill behind the house, and the aviary (which is empty

LAKE ENCHANTO GARDEN

today). There are restrooms on the west side of the ranch house.

Pass the east side of the ranch house and aviary to the signed Peter Strauss Trail. Follow the trail to a signed fork (Peter Strauss Trail), go right at the fork. The trail switchbacks along a densely wooded slope. Stay left at the next fork, on a maintained trail. Herds of mule deer are often seen in the woodlands along the trail. After contouring the shaded ridge for some time, the trail begins to descend down terraced stone steps, through lush fern growth, back to the main trail. Turn left at the main trail, back towards the main ranch house. The trail parallels the ephemeral Triunfo Creek to the right.

SANDSTONE PEAK (3,111') 🐾 CIRCLE X RANCH

Rating: Moderate
Recommended for: Well-conditioned small dogs
Mileage: 1,000' gain, 2.2 miles, 2 hours round-trip
K9 water: 1 quart, no water on route
Posted: Pets on leash. Recommend cleaning up after your pet
Ambience: Classic coastal mountain walk, views across the Pacific
Maps: Automobile Club of Southern California Los Angeles and Vicinity
Hiking Maps: USGS Triunfo Pass 7.5 minute topo, and Trail Map of the Santa Monica Mountains, West
Best time to hike: All year. Summer days can be sweltering. Plan early morning, early evening before sunset. Late winter and spring are the best times to catch wildflowers in bloom. Open daily from 8am to sunset.

DRIVING

From the 101-Ventura Fwy. exit Westlake Blvd.-California 23 South. Drive south on Westlake Blvd./CA 23 South 6.9 miles to Mulholland Highway. Turn right on Mulholland and at 0.3 miles, turn right again on Little Sycamore Canyon Road. Continue on Little Sycamore (which becomes Yerba Buena Road) for 4.3 miles to the Backbone Trail parking lot on the right.

HIKING

From the north end of the parking lot, walk past the information kiosk and locked gate to the Backbone Trail. Follow the trail as it climbs steadily through what is usually dense coastal chaparral and shrub. When this book was first written in 1995, the chaparral and scrub were replaced by the thousands of acres of open, charred terrain as a result of the 1993 firestorm. Despite the fact that everything burned here, there was still an unusual beauty to the terrain. New vegetation has since grown anew bringing spring flowers once again.

Just follow the trail as it switchbacks a few times up to an open, flat area, where the trail is partially paved. To the left (southeast) are steps leading to the summit of Sandstone Peak and a sign which points the way. Walk the steps to a small use trail which traverses over pink volcanic rock, requiring some scrambling, to the summit, marked by a summit register and a monument to W. Herbert Allen.

SUNSET AND SIX CANINES IN THE SHADOWS ON SANDSTONE PEAK

Allen was a major supporter of the Circle X Ranch, which was initially created as a camp for children in the late 1940s.

NOTES

On a clear day, the 360-degree view from the summit of Sandstone Peak is spectacular! Looking southeast across the Pacific Ocean, one can see Santa Catalina, San Clemente, Santa Barbara and San Nicholas islands; to the west, the Channel Islands: Anacapa, Santa Cruz, Santa Rosa and San Miguel. To the north, the peaks of the Los Padres National Forest; to the east, Mt. Baldy in the San Gabriel Mountains and sometimes even San Gorgonio Peak in the San Bernardino Mountains.

LATIGO CANYON TO CASTRO CREST VIA THE BACKBONE TRAIL

Rating: Easy to moderate
Recommended for: Small, well-conditioned dogs
Mileage: 1,030' gain, 4.4 miles, 2.5 hours round-trip on fire road
K9 water: 1 quart, no water on route
Recommend: pets on leash, clean up after your pet
Ambience: Nice view of the San Fernando Valley and San Gabriel Mountains
Maps: Automobile Club of Southern California Los Angeles and Vicinity
Hiking Maps: USGS Point Dume 7.5 minute topo, and Trail Map of the Santa Monica Mountains, West
Best time to hike: All year. Summer days can be sweltering. Plan early morning, early evening before sunset. No shade until the crest.

DRIVING

From the 101-Ventura Freeway, exit Kanan Road and drive south (toward the Pacific Ocean) approximately 6.4 miles to Latigo Canyon Road and turn left. Drive another 2.9 miles to the signed "Backbone Trail" parking area on the left.

HIKING

From the parking area, walk north on the signed "Backbone Trail." Follow the trail up a short rise and then down into the lush, fern-covered upper part of Newton Canyon drainage. The trails drops into the canyon bottom and crosses over ephemeral Newton Creek. On the other side of the creek, the trail begins to climb up the east side of the canyon, eventually leaving the canyon. Follow the trail as it contours along the southern slopes of Castro Peak (identified by all of the radio antennae on the summit) to a saddle, approximately 1.4 miles from the parking area.

At the signed saddle, turn left toward Castro Peak. Hike another 0.8 miles to a second saddle covered by oaks, and where three trails forks converge. This is the end of the hike and lunch can be enjoyed beneath the oaks or on top of a small flat area to the south. The two trails to the left, go within a 0.2 mile of the summit of Castro Peak. The third fork, to the right, can be followed about fifty feet to a flat area on the ridge with great views. The summit of Castro Peak, owned by the County, is closed to the public, however, the view of the San Fernando Valley and San Gabriel Mountains is quite nice. Return to the parking area by the same route.

HAPPINESS ON THE HERMOSA BEACH GREENBELT

Hermosa Beach
HERMOSA TO MANHATTAN BEACH ON THE GREENBELT

Rating: Easy to moderate urban walk
Recommended for: All dogs
Mileage: 4 miles, 1.5 hours round-trip
K9 water: 1 quart, water fountains on route
Posted: Pets on leash, clean up after your pet
Ambience: Nice soft eucalyptus trail, mostly shaded through a garden of exotic trees
Amenities: Water fountains, baggies, trash cans
Maps: Automobile Club of Southern California Los Angeles and Vicinity
Best time to hike: All year

DRIVING
From the 405-Fwy. take the Inglewood Blvd. exit south to 190th Street. Turn right (west) on 190th St. Drive west on 190th St. which becomes Anita Street, then Herondo Street. Continue on Anita/ Herondo as it crosses Pacific Coast Highway about 0.5 miles to Monterey Blvd. Turn right (north) on Monterey, then right on 2nd Street (east), then left on Valley Drive. Follow Valley Drive to the public parking area between 8th and 11th Streets.

HAPPY DOG ON THE GREENBELT

WALKING
Make this hike as long or short as you want. Head north to Manhattan Beach Blvd. on a wonderful shaded walk along an eucalyptus bark trail, soft on dog paws. At Manhattan Beach Blvd. turn around and return by the same route.

THE HISTORIC STRAND

Rating: Easy to moderate urban walk on concrete sidewalk
Recommended for: All dogs
Mileage: varies
K9 water: 1 quart, no water on route (except in public restrooms), no shade
Posted: Pets on leash, clean up after your pet. Dogs are not allowed on the beach or on the Hermosa Pier.
Ambience: Nice in early morning beneath the cool, foggy marine layer or on winter evenings as the sun sets.
Maps: Automobile Club of Southern California Los Angeles and Vicinity
Best time to hike: November to April. Shadeless and hot in midday! Get an early morning start or walk in early evening.

DRIVING

From the 405, exit on Artesia Blvd. west to Pacific Coast Highway. Turn left (south) on PCH and follow to Pier Avenue. Park along Pier Avenue or drive one or two more blocks south then west to Beach Avenue. Park anywhere along Beach Avenue. Look for the walkways on the west side of the street to the Strand.

WALKING

Walk in either direction. Walking south 0.75 miles from Pier Avenue along the Strand takes you to Redondo Beach and King Harbor. Walking north from the pier about 0.25 mile you'll reach Noble Park, a small stretch of green that was the site of the Surf and Sand Club, a private men's club housed in a large hotel-style building built in 1923 and visited by such notables as pilot Charles Lindbergh. After World War II the old club was refurbished and opened as the Hermosa Biltmore Hotel. The hotel was eventually torn down, it's basement filled with sand and converted to a parking lot, before becoming Noble Park.

NOTES

In 1822, the Mexican government granted Antonio Ygnacio Avila a 22,500 acre parcel of land along the south bay coast, later named Rancho Sausal Redondo (ranch of the round grove of willows), that included the Strand.

By the early 1900s, the old rancho had been sold several times over and plans were drawn for the city of Hermosa Beach. A wooden

THE STRAND

boardwalk two miles long ran along Hermosa Beach on what is now the concrete bicycle and walking path. The boardwalk lost many planks to the sea's high tides. Over the years it was replaced with concrete and modified with a low concrete seawall (pictured above).

For almost thirty years, Pacific Electric's Red Cars shuttled passengers from Los Angeles to Santa Monica then down through Manhattan and Hermosa Beach to the Redondo Beach Pier. The concrete path extends from Herondo Street, at the border of Hermosa and Redondo Beach to 45th Street in the north, the border of Manhattan Beach and El Segundo.

The Hermosa Beach pier was built in 1904 three years after the first survey was made for the boardwalk. During a huge storm in 1913, most of the 500 foot wooden pier was swept away. It was demolished to make way for a new pier.

ON THE TRAIL WITH KoKo IN PORTUGUESE BEND

PORTUGUESE BEND ॐ PALOS VERDES PENINSULA

Crenshaw Boulevard is not a street that immediately evokes visions of beauty with its oil refineries, chemical plants, and block after block of industrial and commercially zoned properties. However, follow Crenshaw to its western end in Palos Verdes and it's a different story. Crenshaw Bloulevard deadends at a gate atop coastal bluffs, rolling hills and grasslands with spectacular views of waves breaking across the rocky coast and beyond to Catalina Island. Crenshaw continues beyond the gate as a fire road closed to traffic and is one of the last natural open areas between the densely populated cities of the South Bay and the harbors of San Pedro. Site of the proposed Portuguese Bend Nature Preserve, the entire area includes Barkentine Canyon, and the Forrestal property acquisition, an area of about 1,000 acres.

Like Hawthorne Boulevard to the north, Crenshaw was supposed to end at Palos Verdes Drive. All of those beautiful rolling hills would have been covered with homes if not for one major geological obstacle: a landslide at Portuguese Bend in 1956 just below the end of Crenshaw Boulevard. Today, nearly one-third of the Portuguese Bend Landslide Complex moves about three feet per year! Beneath the topsoil and bedrock is a layer of expanding clay. After a good rain, the clay expands, shifts, and contracts. A favorite study site of college geology classes, this is one of the most geologically fascinating and unstable areas on the peninsula. Between the proposed Portuguese Bend Nature Preserve and Portuguese Point on Palos Verdes Drive is a 0.8 stretch of road where stopping or parking is prohibited due to the unstable geological conditions. This area, just north of Abalone Cove Preserve was the scene of the 1974 Abalone Cove landslide. To this day, property owners are still trying to get the green light for new construction on the remaining vacant parcels.

Occupation of the coast dates back almost 6,500 years to the prehistoric ancestors of the Chumash and Gabrielinos. Portuguese explorer, Juan Rodriguez Cabrillo, passed by "Portuguese Bend" on an expedition to find a passage between the Atlantic and Pacific, but may have not been the first from faraway lands to pass by the coast.

What appear to be stone anchors used by the Chinese on their early ships were found by divers near Malaga Cove.

In 1622, Spanish explorer Sebastiano Vizcaino, who gave San Pedro its name, sailed his flotilla past but never went ashore. Spanish explorer Gaspar De Portola wandered across the Peninsula in 1769, followed a few years later by Spanish missionaries and cattlemen who established trails or claimed their Spanish land grants along California's coast. By the late 1800s, farms and ranches were well established in Los Angeles County and along its coastline. This pastoral scene was to change forever with the onset of World War II.

During the war, the Peninsula served as a strategic military setting. Atop Point Vicente Park at the entrance at 30940 Hawthorne Blvd. are vintage World War II bunkers and a Cold War Nike missile site. The expansion of trails on the bluffside park and building of an interpretive center at Pt. Vicente have been delayed for years due to the discovery of lead contamination on the site from the old gunnery ranges. After World War II, coastal farms were transformed into housing tracts and roads to make way for the families that followed the post-war economic expansion.

Check out www.topozone.com. It is an excellent map resource for this area as well as other areas in the book. They have essentially downloaded all of the USGS quads on their site. As of this writing there are no officially named trails in this area. There is a group called the Palos Verdes Peninsula Land Conservancy that is pushing to get this property acquired for an open space park.

PORTUGUESE BEND HIKES
GENERAL INFORMATION

Rating: Easy to difficult on fire roads and trails
Recommended for: Well-conditioned dogs
Mileage: Varies: 1-10 mile round-trip loops, minimal shade, 1,100'
K9 water: 1 quart, no water on route (except in public restrooms)
Posted: Pets on leash, clean up after your pet
Amenities: Portable restroom currently at first water tank 0.5 miles down fire road
Warnings: Rattlesnakes, ticks
Maps: Automobile Club of Southern California Los Angeles and Vicinity
Hiking Maps: USGS Redondo Beach, San Pedro and Torrance 7.5 minute tops.
On the web: www.topozone.com
Best time to hike: November to April. Summer is hot and shadeless.

DRIVING AND PARKING FROM LAX:

Take the 405 south to Inglewood Blvd. exit. Drive south on Inglewood to 190th, turn right (west). Take 190th to PCH, turn left (south). Follow PCH to Crenshaw Blvd, turn right (west). Follow Crenshaw to its end at a locked gate. Park along the street. Del Cerro Park is on the right (southwest). There is a water fountain at Del Cerro Park for people and dogs but there was no water as of this writing. Carry water with a spare jug in the car.

DRIVING AND PARKING FROM THE 405 SOUTH OR NORTH: Exit on Crenshaw, head west and follow to its end (this is the long way).

HIKING

The end of Crenshaw has long been a favorite for South Bay dog hikers. From the end of Crenshaw, walk past the gate and follow the fire road to foot trails and other fire roads. There is plenty to explore, and getting lost is virtually impossible because of the great visibility, numerous landmarks, neighborhoods, and other trail users.

Depending on the map, the fire roads are either named or not. There has been an ongoing effort to include several areas on south facing side of Palos Verdes Peninsula into one large regional park. Totaling nearly 1,000 acres there are plans for a network of trails and restoration of the native flora. Proposed open space inclusions are Portuguese Bend, the Forrestal property to the southeast and Barkentine Canyon to the northwest. Abalone Cove on the coast, is a marine preserve and dogs are strictly prohibited, even in the parking lot.

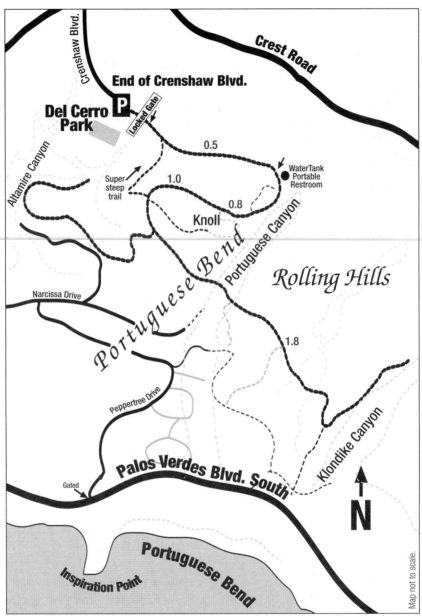

FOR ACCURACY, GET THE USGS REDONDO BEACH, SAN PEDRO AND TORRANCE 7.5 QUADS

The coyotes, fox and other wildlife were driven out of this area a long time ago, but there are plenty of birds to watch including the mourning dove, cactus wren, and California gnatcatcher.

DEL CERRO PARK BLUFF VIEW TO CATALINA

Rating: Easy
Recommended for: Out-of-shape, older or small dogs
Mileage: 0.2 mile round-trip across grass, shaded
K9 water: 1 quart (canine drinking fountain had no water the day it was scouted)
Posted: Pets on leash, clean up after your pet
Ambience: View to Catalina, nice big green lawn
Warnings: Rattlesnakes may be on bluff
Maps: Automobile Club of Southern California Los Angeles and Vicinity
Hiking Maps: USGS Redondo Beach, San Pedro and Torrance 7.5 minute tops.
On the web: www.topozone.com
Best time to hike: All year. Nice in early morning or before sunset on summer days.

WALKING

From your parked car on Crenshaw walk 0.1 mile across the shaded grassy lawn to the bluff overlook to the Pacific. There is a water fountain here for dogs but it wasn't working the day we visited.

PEPPER TREES AND PINES SCENIC LOOP
(Unofficial Name)

Rating: Moderate
Recommended for: Small well-conditioned dogs
Mileage: 1.6 mile round-trip on fire road
K9 water: 1-2 quarts
Posted: Pets on leash, clean up after your pet
Ambience: Lovely walk down gradual fire road and trail with views to Catalina
Warnings: Rattlesnakes, ticks
Maps: Automobile Club of Southern California Los Angeles and Vicinity
Hiking Maps: USGS Redondo Beach, San Pedro and Torrance 7.5 minute tops.
On the web: www.topozone.com
Best time to hike: November to April. Hike early morning or evening in summer.

HIKING

At the end of Crenshaw, walk past the gate on the fire road. Note a trail through brush to the right. Walk about twenty feet on this foot trail and get a fine view of the entire hiking area. This trail, which goes down to the fire road, can be used as a steep 350' variation to the fire road return. Note a knoll covered with pine trees below on the fire road, our destination.

Return to the fire road and follow it down hill 0.5 miles to a grove of old pepper trees, a water tank and a portable restroom. Hidden in this grove, on the last pepper tree on the right, is a lone swing facing the sea, a lovely little spot. Continue on to the knoll of pines approximately 0.3 miles down the road. A foot trail through the tall grass leads to the top and beautiful views to Catalina through the pines (on a clear day). Return the same way or walk north to the steep ridge in full view off to the right (northeast)and follow the foot trail to the top of the fire road.

THE MARINE LAYER MAKES FOR COOL WEATHER ON THE PEPPER TREE AND PINES SCENIC LOOP

CRENSHAW TO PALOS VERDES DRIVE

Rating: Moderate to strenuous
Recommended for: Well-conditioned dogs
Mileage: 6 miles round-trip on fire road, 1,170' of gain on the return
K9 water: 2 quarts, no water
Posted: Pets on leash, clean up after your pet
Ambience: View to Catalina, lovely walks
Warnings: Rattlesnakes, ticks
Maps: Automobile Club of Southern California Los Angeles and Vicinity
Hiking Maps: USGS Redondo Beach, San Pedro and Torrance 7.5 minute tops.
On the web: www.topozone.com
Best time to hike: November to April. Hike early morning or evening in summer.

HIKING

At the end of Crenshaw, walk past the gate on the fire road 0.5 miles to a grove of old pepper trees, a water tank and portable restroom on the left. Hidden in this grove, on the last pepper tree on the right is a swing facing the sea, a lovely little spot. Continue on, passing a beautiful knoll of pines at 0.8 miles. A foot trail through the tall grass leads to the top with beautiful views of Catalina through the pines, on a clear day. The road loops around the knoll and at 1.2 mile forks. Stay right on the fire road. Look behind you for landmarks to be used on the return trip. At 1.5 mile pass Portuguese Canyon. Follow the fire road and any of a myriad of foot paths to any view just above Palos Verdes Drive South. There is a lot to explore in this area and many loop possibilities. The entire landscape presents itself to you, so it is virtually impossible to get lost. Look back on the hike down and make a visual notation of your landmarks. There are many hikers in this area who are very helpful.

Most of Palos Verdes Drive South along the bottom of Portuguese Bend is fenced off. The road is busy and it is not recommended to cross it to the unstable bluffs on the other side. From the bottom of Portuguese Bend, just above Palos Verdes Drive, is an excellent view of geology in action, the effects that earth movement has had on this entire area, the broken cliffs and uneven surfaces jutting up and down. It is an active land mass. Since it's prohibited to park anywhere along this 0.8 mile stretch of roadway which borders Abalone Cove (dogs not allowed) this is the best way to see the landslide.

It's all uphill on the return!

PALOS VERDES ESTATES SHORELINE PRESERVE
PASEO DEL MAR TO CHISWICK ROAD

Rating: Easy
Recommended for: Out-of-shape, older or small dogs
Mileage: 1.25 miles round-trip on bluff foot path, no shade
K9 water: 1 quart, no water on route
Posted: Pets on leash, clean up after your pet
Ambience: View to Catalina
Maps: Automobile Club of Southern California Los Angeles and Vicinity
Hiking Maps: USGS Redondo Beach, San Pedro and Torrance 7.5 minute tops.
On the web: www.topozone.com
Best time to hike: November to April. Hike early morning or evening in summer.

DRIVING

From the intersection of Pacific Coast Highway and Palos Verdes Drive West, drive south on Palos Verdes Drive West approximately 3.3 miles to a "V" intersection with Paseo del Mar, that veers off to the right. Turn immediately right into the public parking lot at this "V" intersection. Park.

WALKING

The Palos Verdes Estates Shoreline Preserve meanders in and out of

neighborhoods from dirt foot path to pavement along the bluff. Follow the dirt path south as it winds along the bluff to a stand of palm trees at Chiswick Road, the end of the path along this portion of bluff. Return the same way.

PINE ALONG THE SHORELINE PRESERVE NEAR CHISWICK ROAD

MUSHIE ABOUT TO HEAD DOWN THE BLUFF PHOTO: DANNY GRAY

THE DOMINATOR

Rating: Moderate. Slippery, steep, dusty path to the beach
Recommended for: Well-conditioned big dogs only!
Mileage: 1.75 miles round-trip on uneven rocky beach path. No shade
K9 water: 1 quart minimum, no water on route
Posted: Pets on leash. Recommend cleaning up after your pet
Ambience: Rugged shoreline beach walk
Warnings: Loose rocky terrain, steep cliffs, not for the faint of heart, human or canine
Maps: Automobile Club of Southern California Los Angeles and Vicinity
Hiking Maps: USGS Redondo Beach, San Pedro 7.5 minute tops.
On the web: www.topozone.com
Best time to hike: All year. Hot and shadeless after 11am.

IMPORTANT NOTES

I love this hike. It is a challenge to find the right route and to hobble along the path of rocks to Rocky Point. The trail down the bluff is not for the faint of heart and the beach walking is uneven, best for big dogs with big paws. Wear shoes with good soles or expect to slip and fall on your bottom and get covered with soft clingy dust.

Despite the fact that homes overlook the entire stretch of beach, access is limited to about three trails, two of which are hair-raising and not for dogs. Ocean on one side and forty feet of bluff on the other makes for an isolated trail, so take friends. Wear a good sturdy pair of trail shoes, carry a cell phone, pack water, lunch or a snack. There is a lot to explore along the beach. There are some incredible reefs along Rocky Point, the very ones that made the Dominator's watery grave!

THE SIGN BELOW THE CLIFF

One of my readers, Danny Gray, first told me about this hike. He asked in disbelief, "You've never hiked down to the Dominator?"

In 1961, the Greek freighter, Dominator, was on its way to Los Angeles Harbor to deliver a load of grain. The crew apparently thought the harbor was just past Rocky Point and turned hard to port right onto the reef (which can be seen from atop the bluff at Paseo del Mar and Epping Road). According to longtime Palos Verdes resident and real estate agent, Dana Graham, friends of hers living in the newly developed tract above Rocky Point heard the tremendous scraping of the freighter's hull as it came across the reef. The wreck soon became a bigger tourist attraction than Marineland south on Long Point. A student then, at Palos Verdes High, Graham said they could smell the fermenting grain on the ocean breeze for weeks.

I wandered two days up and down Paseo del Mar from Malaga to Lunado Coves looking for a suitable trail. The paved beach access from the public parking lot above Malaga Cove is closed to dogs. I finally watched a fellow on the beach with his Rottweiler and Golden Retriever make their way up the cliff. This rugged, challenging coastal hike seems to be a favorite hike for men and their dogs.

MIDWAY DOWN THE TRAIL AT THE MOUTH OF THE CANYON

HEADING NORTH TOWARD ROCKY POINT. THE DOMINATOR IS AROUND THE CORNER.

The nice walking path atop the bluff is part of the unofficial Palos Verdes Estates Shoreline Preserve bluff trail. You can follow this path for miles on the bluff as it parallels Paseo del Mar, weaving its way in and out of neighborhoods, along bike paths and the rugged bluff. There are many "paths" that appear to head down the bluff. Most go for a few feet then dead-end at a cliff.

DRIVING

Take Palos Verdes Drive West to Paseo Lunado. Turn right (west) on Paseo Lunado. On your left (south) note the top of a canyon that will carve deeply to the ocean. This will be the canyon that takes you down to the ocean. Drive approximately 0.9 miles to Avenida Mirola. Note a concrete curb and storm drain on the ocean side across from Avenida Mirola. Turn around and park along the ocean side across from Avenida Mirola facing the way you came. Do not block the driveways of the private residences.

HIKING

From the storm drain to your left, on the bluff foot path, note five posts and a <$iPalos Verdes Estates Shoreline Preserve> sign (landmarks that can change). Walk approximately seventy paces from the

MUSHIE WITH CORMORANTS ON THE HULL OF THE DOMINATOR PHOTO: DANNY GRAY

curb southwest toward the bluff edge, keeping just north of the posts, to a large worn dirt spot on the bluff's edge. Look over the edge of the bluff and down about 12-15 feet for a *Palos Verdes Estates Shoreline Preserve sign*. At this spot, there are two paths down the bluff that merge at the sign as one path down the cliff. Either goes, but the left is easier though steep, slippery with airy views of the canyon and beach. It is the easiest route down the bluffs with the exception of the paved road at Malaga Cove. If you look north along the bluff top about 100 yards, a piece of driftwood marks another route. This one is much easier getting up from the beach than down to the beach.

Follow the trail down to the beach at the mouth of the canyon. Look back at the canyon and note the landmarks. This canyon will be the return path. Wander through a short segment of overgrown trail then turn right (north) toward the point ahead. The beach is rough walking but a path worn down into the rocks is somewhat easier, though not by much. Walk around the bend and the hull of the Dominator comes into view. What appears to be it's cabin is down the beach. Return the same way.

CALLE ENTRADERO AND POINT VICENTE LIGHTHOUSE

Rating: Easy
Recommended for: All dogs
Mileage: 0.1 to 3.0 miles round-trip on nice bluff trail
K9 water: 1 quart, no water
Posted: Pets on leash, clean up after your pet
Ambience: Listen to the lighthouse foghorn on foggy days. A good spot to watch the winter whale migration.
Amenities: Benches, scoop mitts. Public restrooms are 0.25 mile south on Palos Verdes Drive at the Point Vicente Visitor Center
Maps: Automobile Club of Southern California Los Angeles and Vicinity
Best time to hike: All year

DRIVING

Take Hawthorne Blvd. N7 west to Palos Verdes Drive West. The Golden Cove Shopping Center is on the southeast corner. Continue straight across Palos Verdes Drive on Via Vicente which turns to the north and becomes Calle Entradero. Drive about 0.8 mile from Palos Verdes Drive and park along curb on right. As an option, drive about 1.4 miles from Palos Verdes Drive to the public parking lot at what is now the end of Calle Entradero.

HIKING

This wonderful public trail meanders below the newly developed Ocean View Estates along the bluff north of the Point Vicente Lighthouse, a working lighthouse visible from the trail. On foggy days, while sea birds sail by eye-level, the foghorn of the lighthouse can be heard all along the trail as it warns ships to bypass the rocky point. It is a beautiful sound, one that sings of old mariners and tales of the sea. The entire bluff has been revegetated with 17,000 native plants. On a clear day in December, with a good pair of binoculars, you may be able to catch the migration of Pacific gray whales off the coast.

THE POINT VICENTE LIGHTHOUSE FROM THE TRAIL OFF CALLE ENTRADERO

POINT VICENTE LIGHTHOUSE AND PARK

Rating: Easy
Recommended for: All dogs
Mileage: 0.1mile walk on nice bluff. Shaded.
K9 water: 1 quart, no water
Posted: Pets on leash, clean up after your pet
Ambience: Best view of the lighthouse
Amenities: Picnic tables, portable public restroom at time of writing
Maps: Automobile Club of Southern California Los Angeles and Vicinity
Best time to hike: All year

DRIVING

From the intersection Palos Verdes Drive West and Via Vicente drive south about 0.25 mile on Palos Verdes Drive West to a right turn lane (no sign at the time of this writing). This turn lane takes you to the parking lot and temporary headquarters of the Point Vicente Interpretive Center.

WALKING

This is the coastal portion of a much larger park on the site of an old Nike Missile Base on the other side of Pacific Coast Highway. That entrance is at 30940 Hawthorne Blvd. Plans have been in the works for years to build a large interpretive center almost 7,000 square feet and a trail north to connect Point Vicente Park to Ocean View Estates and Calle Entradero.

The entire project came to a standstill several years ago when lead contamination from the old World War II gunnery range was found on the site necessitating removal. Still the projection for the future is positive.

OCEAN TRAILS/PALOS VERDES WEST

Heading south along Palos Verdes South you'll pass Marineland on the right at Long Point. As of this writing, a new coastal bike/waking path is under construction and should be ready by summer 2004.

THE POINT FERMIN LIGHTHOUSE

San Pedro Urban Seaside Walks
POINT FERMIN LIGHTHOUSE AND SUNKEN CITY

Rating: Easy urban walk
Recommended for: All dogs
Mileage: 1.3 miles round-trip. Shaded.
K9 water: 1 quart, no water
Posted: Pets on leash, clean up after your pet
Ambience: Point Fermin Lighthouse, Sunken City and nice views of the Pacific, plenty of shade and sea breeze
Amenities: Picnic tables, restrooms
Maps: Automobile Club of Southern California Los Angeles and Vicinity
Best time to hike: All year

DRIVING AND PARKING

Take the 110-Harbor Fwy. south to the Gaffey Street exit. South on Gaffey to Paseo del Mar and Point Fermin Park. Ample public parking.

WALKING

Walk south on the path to Sunken City, located at the south end of the park. Sunken City is fenced off but people seem to like to wander out there, especially geology classes. The "slump" began in 1929

POINT FERMIN PARK

when waves began to undercut the soft rock beds beneath the coastal bluffs, creating an overhanging or oversteepened condition. People had homes on this section of bluff. Unable to sell their property because of the unstable geologic condition, they continued to live there until 1940 when the slump began to move at a faster rate, breaking into pieces.

Continue around the path overlooking the sea as it loops back to the north. Next point of interest is the Pt. Fermin lighthouse built in 1874. Following the bombing of Pearl Harbor during WWII and subsequent fears of an attack on the west coast, the light was removed and the lighthouse tower was used as a lookout. The building is a beautiful example of Italianate Victorian architecture and is nearing final restoration as of this writing. Though dogs won't be allowed in, it will be worth a quick visit when it is complete.

LOOKING NORTH ACROSS SUNKEN CITY TO POINT FERMIN PARK—
THERE WERE MANY MORE STREETS HERE THIRTY YEARS AGO

POINT FERMIN PARK TO WHITE POINT PARK
ALONG THE HARBOR WALKWAY

Rating: Moderate urban walk
Recommended for: Well-conditioned small dogs
Mileage: 4.4 miles, 3 hours round-trip on sidewalk. No shade near White Point Park.
K9 water: 1 quart minimum, no water (except in public restrooms and water fountains)
Posted: Pets on leash, clean up after your pet
Ambience: Nice walk above the sea to the Point Fermin Lighthouse and Sunken City
Amenities: Picnic tables, restrooms at both parks, and on Paseo del Mar and Meyler St.
Maps: Automobile Club of Southern California Los Angeles and Vicinity
Best time to hike: All year

DRIVING AND PARKING

Take the 110-Harbor Fwy. south to Gaffey Street. South on Gaffey to Paseo del Mar and Point Fermin Park. Plenty of public parking at Point Fermin Park. Scout the route in your car from Point Fermin to White Point Park. You can walk the whole way, turn around any time, or do this as a car shuttle, with a car at either end of the walk.

KoKo HEADS BACK TO POINT FERMIN ALONG THE HARBOR WALKWAY

WALKING

Walk north on the park path along Paseo del Mar. Follow through Point Fermin Park and as it continues about a half mile through a nice San Pedro neighborhood, then opens up again along the bluffs. The route ends at White Point Park/Royal Palms County Beach. At the time of this writing, a new fence was being erected around White Point Park on the east side of Paseo del Mar. At Royal Palms County Beach there are nice picnic tables and restrooms. The walkway continues on about 0.25 mile past the entrance to Royal Palms. Though dogs are not allowed on the county beaches there is plenty to see up on the bluff. White Point Park was in the process of being upgraded at the time of this writing. Check it in the near future for canine hiking potential.

ALTERNATE WALKING VARIATION

Park at Western Avenue-213 and South Paseo del Mar. There is street parking along South Paseo del Mar just before the beginning of the Harbor walkway. It's 2.2 miles from this spot to the Point Fermin Park parking area

KoKo ON THE LONG BEACH DOWNTOWN MARINA WALK TO ISLAND GRISSOM WEST
QUEEN MARY IN THE BACKGROUND

Long Beach
RAINBOW HARBOR URBAN SEASIDE WALKS

Downtown Long Beach and its marina have undergone a massive transition during the past three decades. This part of Long Beach was once really creepy. For most of the 20th century, the Pike, an amusement park built in the early 1900s when Long Beach was a lovely resort destination, covered what is now the Downtown Long Beach Marina area. Old, crumbling and decrepit by 1970, the Pike's glory days had long passed. The entire area attracted the human flotsam and jetsam of the coastal subculture: derelicts, drug addicts, ruffians and unsavory characters, though my mother warned my sister and I not to go there because of the sailors!

The sun finally set for the the last time on the Pike in 1979. Demolition of buildings began and the Pike closed forever. The City of Long Beach spent the next three decades redesigning and renovating the area, a massive undertaking that has paid off well. It's not the same place it was thirty years ago, even five years ago. There are still a few vague holdouts from the past, but these too are quickly disappearing as real estate values in Southern California escalate.

SHORELINE HARBOR MARINA TO ISLAND GRISSOM NORTH

Rating: Easy urban walk
Recommended for: All dogs
Mileage: 0.5 mile walk along quay to its end across from Island Grissom, no shade
K9 water: 1 quart, no water
Posted: Pets on leash, clean up after your pet
Ambience: Nice view of marina, harbor and the "long beach"
Amenities: Public parking and restrooms
Maps: Automobile Club of Southern California Los Angeles and Vicinity
Best time to hike: October to April. Early mornings or evenings before sunset on cooler summer days

DRIVING

Take the 405 Fwy. to 710 Fwy. west. Exit on Shoreline Drive and go east to Linden Avenue. Turn south on Linden into the Shoreline Harbor Marina parking lot, the northeast end of the Downtown Long Beach Marina on your Thomas Guide.

PARKING

Park in the south end of the lot near the restroom. This lot is either

parking by permit for the boat owners or public parking with a paid stub displayed on the windshield of your car.

Note the yellow computerized "pay stations" scattered across the perimeter of the lot. Pick a space, note your space number and get your parking stub at the pay station. A talking computer will guide you through the steps. It's about one dollar per hour and the machine takes quarters and dollar bills.

WALKING

From the south end of the parking lot, where the last row of boats in the marina meets the sea, walk southeast on the "quay" toward a 1960s modernesque tower that is actually a camouflaged oil drilling rig on man made, Island Grissom. On one side of the asphalt path is the marina, on the other, the north end of the "long beach." The path ends at favorite fishing spot on the rocks just across from Island Grissom.

SHORELINE HARBOR MARINA
TO THE DOWNTOWN LONG BEACH MARINA

Rating: Easy to moderate urban walk
Recommended for: Well-conditioned small dogs
Mileage: 1.3 miles round-trip, no shade
K9 water: 1 quart, no water
Posted: Pets on leash, clean up after your pet
Ambience: Nice view of marina
Amenities: Public parking and restrooms
Maps: Automobile Club of Southern California Los Angeles and Vicinity
Best time to hike: October to April. Early mornings or evenings before sunset on cooler summer days

DRIVING

PARKER'S WITH THE LIONS LIGHTHOUSE FOR SIGHT IN THE BACKGROUND

Take the 405 to 710 Fwy. west. Exit West Shoreline Drive south to Linden Avenue. Turn west on Linden Avenue into the Shoreline Harbor parking lot.

WALKING

From the parking lot walk over to the bike/walking path next to the boat marina. Follow this path west, with the Marina on your left. Pass Shoreline Village on your right, you'll come to the parking lot entrance of the Downtown Long Beach Marina. There are benches, a large grassy area, shade, great views of the Queen Mary across Queensway Bay, the Long Beach Lions Lighthouse for Sight and Parker's Lighthouse Restaurant. This lighthouse was a gift to the City of Long Beach. It stands at 65-feet hand has two 750-watt rotating lamps to guide boats into the harbor. Return the same way.

DOWNTOWN LONG BEACH MARINA TO ISLAND GRISSOM WEST

Rating: Easy to moderate urban walk
Recommended for: Well-conditioned small dogs
Mileage: 1 mile round-trip, shade
K9 water: 1 quart, no water
Posted: Pets on leash, clean up after your pet
Ambience: Nice view of marina
Amenities: Public parking and restrooms
Maps: Automobile Club of Southern California Los Angeles and Vicinity
Best time to hike: October to April. Early mornings or evenings before sunset on cooler summer days

DRIVING

Take the 405 to 710 Fwy. west. Exit West Shoreline Drive south to Shoreline Village Drive. Turn south on Shoreline Village drive then

right into the Shoreline Village public parking lot (about one dollar per hour). There are very few metered space in the marina parking lot. Most spaces are for boat owners.

WALKING

Lots of sniffing potential on this walk. From Shoreline Village walk south across the street to the sidewalk that starts next to Parker's Restaurant, the red-roofed building that looks like the Coronado Hotel on Coronado Island near San Diego. Follow the path along the harbor with the boat marina on your left.

Long Beach and its marinas have served as locations for many films. Clint Eastwood spent three weeks here shooting "Blood Work" aboard the trawler, The Grand Banks 42 (called, *The Following Sea*, in the film) at Gangway G.

There are nice grassy spots and shade most of the way with great views of the Queen Mary across the harbor on your right. Walk to the end for views of Long Beach Outer Harbor to the Pacific. Return the same way or along the marina side.

THE AUTHOR AND SYD ON THE ROAD TO VETTER MOUNTAIN

THE SAN GABRIEL MOUNTAINS

The San Gabriel Mountains are the beautiful yet formidable wall of decomposing granite that separates the Los Angeles Basin from the Mojave Desert. The highest point is 10,064', the summit of Mount San Antonio, "Old Baldy." On summer afternoons spectacular thunderheads gather above the crest and can be seen from as far south as Rancho Palos Verdes. From the valleys below, steep ridges and crumbling boulder-filled canyons appear impassable. From end to end, there are endless opportunities for dog hiking on meandering pine-covered ridges and trails.

The earliest prehistoric visitors to the San Gabriel Mountains came thousands of years ago. Their descendants, the Gabrielino, Serrano and Fernandino Indians watched Spanish explorers search for new routes across the mountain passes. Soon after, Spanish missionaries followed. California's gold rush of 1848, brought miners and pioneers who crossed the continent to find their fortunes. Many settled along the western edge of the San Gabriels cutting the timber and collecting streambed rocks to build homes. Ranchers and homeowners fought for the rights to the water that came down the canyons of the San Gabriels.

A diverse collection of flora, shrubs and trees called chaparral can be found in the San Gabriel foothills: yucca, wild lilac, mountain mahogany, laurel and manzanita. At higher elevations above the chaparral are forests of pine, Jeffrey, ponderosa, Coulter, lodgepole, incense cedar and white fir.

Mule deer, a small population of black bears and mountain lions, bighorn sheep, coyotes, fox, chipmunks, squirrels, skunks, raccoons, bobcats, and weasels are among the population of mammals that make a home in this natural land island between freeways. Human encroachment has had a devastating effect on wildlife populations with larger mammals attempting to avoid contact with people altogether. Give them their space. This is their home.

Though the San Gabriel Mountains are easily accessible from Los Angeles, trailheads and trails are isolated. Cell phones may not always get reception in the canyons. Cell phones get limited reception, mostly on high points. Carry the right equipment, plenty of water, food, rain gear and be prepared. Know where the ranger stations and public phones are.

The weather can change at any time, from sunshine and blue sky to the thunder and lightning of a sudden storm. Having this happen while walking on an exposed ridge trail can be quite disconcerting. Avoid cutting switchbacks (short-cutting) on mountain trails. Switchbacks erode trails physically and visually. The San Gabriel Mountains are a gift to the City of Angels. Each of us can be a steward for their protection.

ADVENTURE PASS (http://www.fsadventurepass.org/)

An Adventure Pass must be displayed in all vehicles parked within the Angeles, Los Padres, San Bernardino, and Cleveland National Forests. The purpose of the pass is to help defray USFS operational costs and to improve recreational opportunities for all of us.

Annual or daily passes can be purchased from USFS offices, sporting good stores, local shops, gas stations near forest entry points, or by mail from the USFS. The website address above lists stores that sell the pass.

The USFS also sells recreation maps, and provides free information pamphlets on many different subjects. Maps show the trails, dirt roads, campgrounds, landmarks and other points of interest. Maps, passes and additional information can be obtained from the USFS by calling or visiting one of their offices.

USFS RANGER STATION CONTACTS:

Angeles National Forest Headquarters
701 N. Santa Anita
Arcadia, CA 91006
(626) 574-1613
http://www.r5fs.fed.us/angeles

Arroyo-Seco Ranger District
Oak Grove Park
Flintridge, CA 91011
(626) 790-1151

Los Angeles River Ranger District
12371 N. Little Tujunga Cyn. Rd.
San Fernando, CA 91342
(818) 899-1900

San Gabriel River Ranger District
110 N. Wabash
Glendora, CA 91741
(626) 335-1251

STREAM AND TERRACED FLOOD CONTROL ALONG THE SISTER ELSIE TRAIL-
OLD JET PROPULSION LAB ROAD

GOULD MESA TO ARROYO SECO

Rating: Moderate.
Recommended for: Small well-conditioned dogs
Mileage: 700' of gain, 4.5 miles, 2-3 hours round-trip on fire road
K9 water: Water in stream on route, carry 1 quart
Posted: Pets on leash. Recommend cleaning up after your pet
Ambience: Beautiful walk through cool canyon with stream
Maps: Automobile Club of Southern California Los Angeles and Vicinity
Hiking maps: USGS Arroyo Seco 7.5 minute topo
Best time to hike: Year-round. Do not hike during heavy rains or high water.

DRIVING

Take the 210 Fwy. to the 2-Angeles Crest Highway in La Canada and exit. Drive north on Angeles Crest Highway approximately 2 miles to a dirt parking area on the right side of the road, just above the La Canada-Flintridge Country Club.

THE AUTHOR AND GEOLOGIST ANDY ZDON WITH SYD AND K.D. IN THE ARROYO SECO

HIKING

Park and walk a few feet to the driveway just above the parking area. Follow the paved driveway past a locked gate passing the electric humming of the Gould Substation on your right, named after 19th century Arroyo homesteader, Will Gould. The paved road climbs a short, steep hill, then quickly descends into the canyon of the Arroyo Seco. The road soon turns to dirt after passing beneath a stately oak tree. This is the old Gould Mountain Way.

About 1.3 miles from Angeles Crest Highway, the dirt road reaches the bottom of the canyon, the old Arroyo Seco Road, the USFS Angeles National Forest boundary and Gould Mesa Campground (there is a restroom), a favorite camp with mountain bikers. This location is about 3.25 miles above Nasa's Jet Propulsion Lab.

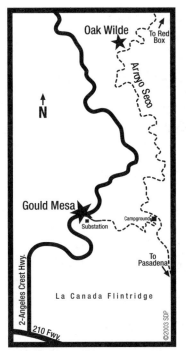

At Gould Mesa, the road forks. To the left, the historic dirt road continues up the Arroyo to Paul Little Picnic Area (0.7 miles, one-way), the Oak Wilde Campground (3.2 miles one-way), eventually reaching Switzer's Camp and Eaton Saddle. Turn right and follow the road as it meanders through the canyon, paralleling the creek. Note an old gauging station and cabin ruins on either side of the creek. Follow the dirt road past several bridges to the southern boundary of the Angeles National Forest. Return by the same route.

NOTES

A wonderful conditioning hike for dogs readying for more difficult conquests, the Arroyo is fragrant with the sweet smell of old moist leaves and sagebrush. With the exception of the first mile, the hike is fairly flat, with numerous stream crossings. The stream can be fairly deep during winter and completely impassable in heavy rains.

The canyons of the San Gabriel Mountains literally drain hundreds of square miles of mountain terrain. These mountains have been carved by the erosive forces of nature. Throughout recorded history, disastrous floods and debris flows, water filled with rocks and mud, have crashed down the western slopes and canyons to the sea. The worst of these, during the past century, occurred in 1938 and 1969. Floods ravaged the landscape, destroying complete neighborhoods all along the Los Angeles River Basin, with a great loss of life. Installation of debris catch basins at the mouth of all drainages in the San Gabriels minimized the catastrophic damage of these past floods by catching the rocks in the debris flow, allowing water to flow down the storm channels. However, the basins are at the bottom of the canyons, not in them!

GOULD MESA TO OAK WILDE

Rating: Moderate
Recommended for: Small well-conditioned dogs
Mileage: 1,300' of gain, 9 miles, 4-5 hours round-trip on fire road, narrow trail with at least 15 stream crossings.
K9 water: Water in stream on route, carry 1 quart
Posted: Pets on leash. Recommend cleaning up after your pet
Amenities: Beautiful walk through resort ruins where movie stars like Clark Gable, Joan Crawford and Mary Pickford once stayed
Maps: Automobile Club of Southern California Los Angeles and Vicinity
Hiking maps: USGS Arroyo Seco 7.5 minute topo
Best time to hike: Year-round. Do not hike during heavy rains or high water.

DRIVING

Take the 210 Fwy. to 2-Angeles Crest Highway in La Canada and exit. Drive north on Angeles Crest Highway approximately 2 miles to a dirt parking area on the right side of the road, just above the La Canada-Flintridge Country Club.

HIKING

Park and walk a few feet to the driveway just above the parking area. Follow the paved driveway past a locked gate passing the humming Gould Substation (named after 19th century Arroyo homesteader, Will Gould). The paved road climbs a short, steep hill, then quickly descends into the canyon of the Arroyo Seco. The road soon turns to dirt after passing beneath a stately oak tree.

About 1.3 miles from Angeles Crest Highway, the dirt road reaches the bottom of the canyon, the old Arroyo Seco Road, the USFS Angeles National Forest boundary and Gould Mesa Campground (there is a restroom), a favorite camp with mountain bikers. At Gould Mesa, the road forks. To the left, the historic dirt road continues up the Arroyo Seco to Paul Little Picnic Area (0.7 miles, one-way), the Oak Wilde Campground (3.2 miles one-way), eventually reaching Switzer's Camp and beyond that, Eaton Saddle.

Turn left up the canyon, paralleling the creek to your right. Along the trail are the stone foundations of mountain cabins built around the turn of the century. Many of these stone ruins can be spotted amidst groves of decades-old cactus and century plants. English Ivy, purple vinca and paper whites are all that's left of the gardens planted by the canyon dwellers before the great flood of 1938. About fifteen minutes from Gould Mesa Campground, you'll pass Niño Campground on the left. Approximately 1.7 miles (and about nine boot-soaking stream crossings) from the Gould Mesa Campground, you'll reach Paul Little Picnic Area. At the picnic area, the trail forks. To the right, is the Gabrielino Trail which continues on to Oak Wilde. To the left is the picnic area, a pit restroom and a use trail which leads to the base of the Brown Canyon Debris Basin. Stop and rest at one of the tables set on terraced slopes over-looking the Arroyo.

Continue from the picnic area on the trail fork to the right, which climbs and traverses a steep ridge before dropping back into the arroyo. From this trail, look down upon the Brown Canyon Debris Basin. Once back in the canyon, follow the trail as it zigzags back and forth, across a sandy wash (and many more stream crossings), finally reaching Oak Wilde campground. Relax and enjoy the sounds of the canyon from one of the many picnic tables. Notice a huge oleander and an old lemon tree, all that remains of the garden plantings from the early days. Return to Gould Mesa by the same route.

NOTES

As early as 1884, there was a mountain resort established high in the canyon known as Switzer's Camp, and by 1911 a tourist camp was built at what is now Oak Wilde Campground. Since the late 1800s, thousands of visitors traveled this dirt road up the canyon. Some of the famous visitors who signed the guest register at Switzer's included Clark Gable, Mary Pickford, Henry Ford, Joan Crawford and Shirley Temple. By 1935, the USFS recorded at least 127 privately-owned cabins (on leased USFS land) in the lower Arroyo Seco Canyon.

The Great Flood of 1938 and subsequent floods since then, washed away many of the cabins, the old road, and changed the course of the stream on more than one occasion. Evidence of this is the Elmer Smith Bridge (south of Gould Mesa Campground) which, at the time of this writing, was suspended over a dry channel with a "no fishing from bridge" sign hanging from the bridge. Arroyo Seco was the Spanish name for dry brook which perhaps, is a more accurate description for the section of the Arroyo below Devil's Gate Reservoir.

HAINES CANYON STREAMSIDE 🐾 SISTER ELSIE TRAIL

Rating: Easy to moderate
Recommended for: Small well-conditioned dogs
Mileage: 350' of gain, 2.25 miles, 1-1.5 hours round-trip on fire road and trail
K9 water: 1 quart minimum, water in stream on route
Posted: Pets on leash. Recommend: cleaning up after your pet
Ambience: Historic trail walk follows portions of the old Sister Elsie and JPL trails
Maps: Automobile Club of Southern California Los Angeles and Vicinity
Hiking maps: USGS Sunland and Condor Peak 7.5 minute topos
Best time to hike: Year-round. Early morning or late afternoon in summer.

DRIVING

Take the 210 Fwy. and exit on Lowell Avenue. Follow Lowell north past Foothill Blvd to Day Street. Turn left (west) on Day Street and follow to Haines Canyon. Turn right (north) on Haines Canyon and park below Apperson Street. In February 2000, no parking signs were installed at the end of Haines Canyon. Parking was always tight at the end of the block and residents were tired of cars blocking their driveways. For over fifty years Haines Canyon, the Sister Elsie Trail, has been a popular route up Mt. Lukens for one of the Sierra Club's oldest climbing sections, the Hundred Peaks Section.

HIKING

Walk up Haines Canyon, which turns to dirt at the end of the pavement, passing private residences on the left and the fenced Haines Canyon Debris Basin on the right. During the flood of 1969, this debris basin, like so many others in the San Gabriels, filled up with rocks and debris that washed down the canyons. The basin filled up with rocks so quickly, that the City of Los Angeles wasn't able to empty it fast enough. Consequently, it over-topped, flooding the streets below.

Walk past a locked gate and follow the main fire road, staying right at the first two forks within first 1/4 mile. The fork just above the debris basin is the Graveyard Truck Trail and can be followed all the way to the old Tujunga Graveyard atop Parsons Trail. This is the place where, during the rains of 1969, the earth gave way and caskets, bodies and bones washed down into the neighborhood below.

AFTER THE 1938 FLOOD: REMAINS OF AN OLD CABIN FIRELPLACE IN HAINES CANYON

The drainage on the right, parallels the road all the way up the canyon. At about 3/4 mile, pass a grove of sycamore trees and the ruins of a cabin on a terrace above the trees. Although not visible from the road, the ruins are accessible from the road by a small footpath. Continue on the fire road, until you reach a large boulder strewn wash that crosses the road. Sometimes water is flowing across the road here. Turn right at the fork just on the other side of the wash and walk past a gate. The Sister Elsie Trail continues up the wash but is quite overgrown and hard to follow. About twenty feet past the gate on the right, is a well-worn use trail that drops back down into the lush fern-covered drainage of Haines Canyon. Watch for poison oak along the way. Follow the trail back to the small plateau just above the debris basin pond, careful not to wander off onto one of the many forks to the left which will take you into Blue Gum Canyon, the next drainage to the east. When you reach the plateau, walk back to the fire road and follow it back down to Haines Canyon.

NOTES

Haines Canyon is located at the foot of Mt. Lukens in the heart of Tujunga, the name given by the Spaniards to the Gabrielino Indians who had established a large settlement here. In 1840, the Mexican government granted approximately 6,600 acres, Rancho Tujunga, to brothers Pedro and Francisco Lopez. By 1885, Tujunga's first post office was established, followed by the Tujunga School district in 1888 and the early agricultural cooperative community of Little Lands in the early 1900s. By the 1920s and 30s, Tujunga became famous for its excellent air quality and many health sanitariums were located there. Foundations of the old sanitariums, long abandoned, can still be found just above Day Street in the foothills.

By the 1960s, Tujunga's demographics had changed radically, earning it the nickname "The Rock" (as in Alcatraz) from the Los Angeles Police Department. Before the 210 Freeway was built, the only way in and out of Tujunga was by Foothill Boulevard. Tujunga became the perfect hideaway spot for motorcycle gangs, meth labs, pot growers and artists (oh, the poor artists!). During the real estate boom of the late 1980s, most of the bikers, approaching their sixties, moved north to the periphery of the Mojave Desert, to the communities of Lancaster and Palmdale. There are still a few holdouts from the 1960s.

California bungalows and stone hunting cabins from the days of Little Lands, are sandwiched in between new homes. This contrast in real estate and history can be seen on many Tujunga streets especially on Glory, one block west from Haines Canyon between Apperson and Day Street. On one side of the street is a row of tiny clapboard cabins while on the other, three-quarter of a million dollar homes.

There are some old cabin ruins in Haines Canyon with great fireplaces made of stream bed stones in the wash, victims of the great flood of 1938 and subsequent fires. Purple vinca and English ivy are all that's left of the gardens planted by the early canyon settlers.

In the spring, local residents of Armenian descent pick the stinging nettles in the canyon for cooking in homeland recipes. You might meet them along the way carrying bags full of freshly picked nettles, however, we definitely suggest that you don't pick the nettles or any other plant in the area (and certainly don't eat them!). Stinging nettles are mighty unpleasant if touched by people or dogs and cause a long-lasting, burning rash. The fire road and trail are also used by equestrians from the local area.

MT. LUKENS FROM HAINES CANYON

Rating: STRENUOUS!
Recommended for: Well-conditioned dogs only!!
Mileage: 3,000' of gain, 9 miles, 6-8 hours round-trip on fire road and trail
K9 water: Carry 2 quarts minimum, no shade above canyon
Posted: Pets on leash. Recommend cleaning up after your pet
Ambience: Fabulous view of Los Angeles and San Gabriels
Maps: Automobile Club of Southern California Los Angeles and Vicinity
Hiking maps: USGS Sunland and Condor Peak 7.5 minute topos
Best time to hike: October to April. Get an early morning start.

DRIVING

Take the 210 Fwy. and exit on Lowell Avenue. Follow Lowell north past Foothill Blvd to Day Street. Turn left (west) on Day Street. Follow Day to Haines Canyon Avenue. Turn right (north) on Haines Canyon. There are now no parking signs the last block before the trailhead, so park along Haines Canyon below Apperson Street.

HIKING

Walk up Haines Canyon, which turns to dirt at the end of the pavement, passing though a gate and by private residences. You'll pass two forks on the left, the first a private driveway. The second, just above the debris basin on your right, is the old Graveyard Truck Trail that ends at a detention center on Big Tujunga Canyon Road, but not before passing the old cemetery at the top of Parsons Trail. During the flood of 1969, part of the graveyard hillside collapsed sending coffins and skeletons all the way down to Von's parking lot (so they say) on Foothill Blvd. The Haines Canyon debris basin like so many others in the San Gabriels, overtopped, and flooded the streets below.

About a mile above the debris basin, the fire road forks. The right fork continues up Haines Canyon to an overgrown spring and is the old overgrown Sister Elsie Trail. Stay left on the main fire road, eventually passing through a locked gate. Follow the fire road as it climbs steadily up the canyon to the summit of the peak. There is no shade once you leave the canyon so an early start is imperative.

There are a number of electronic installations on the summit, however, these do not interfere with the spectacular view of the Big Tujunga watershed, and (on a clear day) all the way across the Los Angeles basin out to

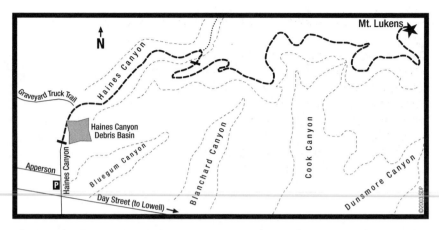

the Pacific Ocean. Mt. Lukens is very popular with mountain bikers who ride up from Angeles Crest Highway to the east.

ALTERNATE HIKING ROUTE FROM ANGELES CREST HIGHWAY

Mileage: 2,200' of gain, 10 miles, 7 hours round-trip on fire road and trail

5.3 miles north of the 210 Fwy. on Angeles Crest Hwy. is a dirt parking area on the left side. From the south end of the parking area follow a trail to a junction with USFS road 2N80. Go left (SW) on 2N80 to 2N76. Go right (NW) on 2N76 all the way to the summit.

NOTES

The hike to Mt. Lukens from Haines Canyon amidst the fragrant aromas of the chaparral, up the old JPL fire road, is a good aerobic workout for canines and their owners preparing for more significant endeavors. In the canyon are a number of old cabin sites, the stone foundations of which are covered with English ivy, purple vinca and native flora. One of the most interesting of these sites is perched on a hillside above a grove of sycamores, only about a mile up the canyon. During the summer, the dirt road can be very hot and dusty, so an early morning start is recommended.

Mt. Lukens is the highest mountain within Los Angeles City limits and was originally named by the U.S. Army's Wheeler Survey topographers "Sister Elsie Peak" after a Catholic nun who ran an orphanage for Native American children. In the twenties, the peak was renamed for Theodore P. Lukens, mayor of Pasadena in 1894, noted for his reforestation efforts. The fire lookout built on the summit by the USFS in 1927, was moved to Josephine Peak in 1937.

MT. LOWE (5,603') FROM EATON SADDLE

Rating: Moderate
Recommended for: Small well-conditioned dogs
Mileage: 500' of gain, 3 miles, 2 hours round-trip on fire road and trail
K9 water: 1 quart minimum, no water on route
Suggested: Pets on leash. Recommend cleaning up after your pet
Amenities: Historic hike, breathtaking view of Los Angeles to Catalina Island
Maps: Automobile Club of Southern California Los Angeles and Vicinity
Hiking maps: USGS Mount Wilson 7.5 minute topo
Best time to hike: Year-round. Best weather from April to November.

The Mt. Wilson road is open year-round, but may be closed on occasion due to rock slides or snow. Recommend leashing dogs from the parking area at Eaton Saddle until the Mueller Tunnel as there are steep cliffs along that portion of the road.

DRIVING

Take the 210 Fwy. to the 2-Angeles Crest Highway in La Canada and exit. Drive north on Angeles Crest Highway approximately 14 miles to Red Box. Turn right on the Mt. Wilson Road. Drive 2.3 miles to Eaton Saddle. Park in a large dirt parking area, careful not to block the locked gate.

HIKING

Walk past the locked gate and follow the dirt road, passing sheer drop-offs to your left and steep walls to your right. Pass through the Mueller Tunnel, named for A. J. "Hap" Mueller, who beginning in 1925, was charged with building an elaborate network of firebreaks and fire roads for the United States Forest Service in the San Gabriel Mountains. Just before you enter the tunnel, look at the cliffs just to the left and slightly above the tunnel. There are some old railings clinging to the rocky precipice, stoic reminders of the original hair-raising trail to Mt. Lowe before the road and tunnel were built by the Forest Service. Continue on to Markham Saddle. At Markham Saddle the road starts to head downhill, off to the right. Leave the road at the saddle by turning left onto a foot path (USFS trail 12W14), which quickly rises above the road, paralleling it for some time, through oaks and chaparral. Follow this pleasant trail to a saddle between Mt. Markham and Mt. Lowe. Continue south past the saddle approximately 200 yards to a junction. Turn right (west) on the trail which will take you to the summit of Mt. Lowe.

THE MUELLER TUNNEL ON THE TRAIL TO MT. LOWE FROM EATON SADDLE

NOTES

The history of Mt. Lowe is certainly one of the most colorful of all the peaks in the San Gabriel Mountains. In 1891, funded by Professor Thaddeus Lowe from Pasadena, construction began on the Mt. Lowe Railway. At that time, it was considered to be one of the engineering wonders of the world. Collaborating with engineer David Joseph Macpherson, who located the rail route, Lowe built the first electrically-powered incline mountain railway in the world.

In 1892, while the railway was under construction, Lowe escorted, on horseback, a group of VIPs from Pasadena on a tour of the area. The trip ended on what was then known as Oak Mountain. As the group stood on the summit of the peak, someone proposed renaming the peak Mt. Lowe, in honor of their guide and host. Everyone present thought it was a great idea, and so Mt. Lowe came to be.

From 1893 to 1935, during the peak years of operation for the Mt. Lowe Railway, thousands of people rode the railway from Mountain Junction in Altadena, 1,300' to Echo Mountain. There they found a hotel, a casino-dance hall, a zoo, an observatory, several residences, a power plant and the "Great Searchlight," which was then, the world's largest searchlight. In 1895, "Ye Alpine Tavern" was formally opened 1,000' below the summit of Mt. Lowe. From the tavern, visitors could ride the guided "pony train" or hike on two-well maintained trails to the summit of Mt. Lowe. Unfortunately, beginning as early as 1900, a series of disastrous fires, subsequent floods and other ill-fated events, all but eradicated any trace of the mountain's glorious past.

The trail from Eaton Saddle to Mt. Lowe tends to be hot and dusty during the summer months, but oak trees along the trail and near the summit provide some shade. The trail to Mt. Lowe is very popular and well-traveled. On a clear day, there are great views of the Los Angeles basin, out to the Pacific ocean and Catalina Island.

JOSEPHINE PEAK (5,558')

Rating: Moderate.
Recommended for: Rigorous challenge for small well-conditioned dogs.
Mileage: 1,900' of gain, 8 miles, 5.5 hours round-trip on fire road
K9 water: 2 quarts minimum, no water on route
Ambience: Beautiful views of the San Gabriels and Strawberry Peak
Maps: Automobile Club of Southern California Los Angeles and Vicinity
Hiking maps: USGS Condor Peak 7.5 minute topo
Best time to hike: Late September to early May. Hot in summer. Some snow in winter.

DRIVING

Take the 210 Fwy. to the 2-Angeles Crest Highway in La Canada and exit. Drive north on Angeles Crest Highway approximately 9.5 miles to the Angeles Forest Highway (N3). Turn left (north) and park in the dirt parking area on the west side of Angeles Forest Highway.

HIKING

Cross the highway to a dirt road on the east side of Angeles Forest Highway. Follow the dirt road as it meanders up some switchbacks, two miles to a junction. From this junction, you have a beautiful view to the east of Strawberry Peak, across Josephine Saddle. To the west, is the route to Josephine Peak. Continue to the left (west) up the fire road, to the summit of Josephine Peak. All that is left of the old fire lookout, a concrete foundation, marks the summit.

NOTES

Josephine Peak is best hiked during mild weather. There is no shade along the road with the exception of a few pine trees near the summit. In 1937, a fire lookout was constructed on the summit and remained in service until it burned down in 1976. Josephine Peak was named after Josephine Lippencott who was married to USGS surveyor Joseph Barlow Lippencott. In 1894, Lippencott used Josephine Peak as a survey station.

STRAWBERRY PEAK (6,164')

Rating: Moderate-strenuous.
Recommended for: Rigorous challenge for small well-conditioned dogs.
Mileage: 1,500' of gain, 6 miles, 5-6 hours round-trip on trail
K9 water: 2 quarts minimum, no water on route
Ambience: Beautiful views of San Gabriels, historic walk.
Maps: Automobile Club of Southern California Los Angeles and Vicinity
Hiking maps: USGS Condor Peak and Chilao Flat 7.5 minute topos
Best time to hike: October to May. Hot in summer. Some snow and ice on trail in winter.

DRIVING

Take the 210 Fwy. to the 2-Angeles Crest Highway in La Canada and exit. Drive north on Angeles Crest Highway approximately 14 miles to Red Box. Park in paved parking area just off Angeles Crest Highway.

HIKING

From the parking area, cross the highway and walk east approximately 100' to a dirt road on the left (2N46). Walk the dirt road as it parallels the highway for about 0.75 mile to a junction with a trail on the left. Turn left and follow the trail, through thick chaparral, about 0.25 mile to the top of a ridge rising up from Red Box.

Follow the trail in a northerly direction, as it winds its way around Mount Lawlor on the right, to the saddle between Mount Lawlor and Strawberry Peak. From this point, the trail starts to descend the east side of the ridge. Leave the main trail, and follow a use trail to the north, along the ridge and over some ups and downs, then switchbacking steeply upward to the prominent summit of Strawberry Peak.

NOTES

Strawberry Peak is most comfortably hiked with canines during the spring and late fall, when the daytime temperature is moderate. The hike can be sweltering during the summer months. Like many other peaks in the San Gabriel mountains, there is little or no shade. Extra water should be carried.

According to Hiram Reid, who chronicled the early history of Pasadena and environs during the late 19th century, Strawberry Peak was affectionately named by "some wags at Switzer's Camp," because of the massive summit which, from various vistas, somewhat resembled a strawberry. Our favorite true story about Strawberry Peak took place in 1909 when the Grand Army of the Republic was sponsoring a week-long fair in Pasadena which offered, among the many amusements, balloon rides in Captain A.E. Mueller's giant gas balloon, America. One afternoon with high clouds overhead, Captain Mueller was taking the usual half-dozen passengers for a ride when, to the horror of the fair-going public, the balloon was snapped up by an air current and disappeared into the clouds. Reaching elevations as high as 14,000', the balloon and its terrified male passengers traveled through snow and rain. Just before nightfall, the Captain spotted grey boulders through the clouds and brought the balloon down upon the snowy summit of Strawberry Peak.

After spending a damp night huddled around a small fire trying to stay warm in the falling snow, the men wandered about the summit of the peak, looking off in every direction for some sign of life. They spotted a thin wisp of smoke coming from the chimney of a small snow-covered cabin some distance away. Greatly relieved in knowing that their predicament might soon end, they headed for the cabin through knee-deep snow. When they arrived at the cabin, they were greeted by early San Gabriel Mountain pioneers, Ma and Pa Colby, who dried their clothes and served them a hot meal while listening to their incredible story. The following day, Pa Colby led the group down the steep, snow-covered ridges to Switzer's Camp, where after a short rest, they made the long-awaited descent into the Arroyo Seco where family, friends, reporters and well-wishers waited. From the moment their hot-air balloon disappeared into the clouds above the San Gabriels, their story was front-page news across the country.

SPECTACULAR VISTAS FROM VETTER MOUNTAIN

VETTER MOUNTAIN LOOKOUT (5,908')

Rating: Easy.
Recommended for: Out-of-shape, older and small dogs
Mileage: 300' of gain,1.25 miles, 2 hours round-trip on fire road
K9 water: 1 quart minimum, no water on route
Ambience: Beautiful views of San Gabriels, historic fire lookout
Maps: Automobile Club of Southern California Los Angeles and Vicinity
Hiking maps: USGS Chilao Flat 7.5 minute topo
Best time to hike: April to November. Hot in summer. USFS road 3N16 is closed at Angeles Crest Highway in Winter. The fire road to the peak can be hiked from Angeles Forest Highway in winter, but tends to be icy.

DRIVING
Take the 210 Freeway to the 2-Angeles Crest Highway in La Canada and exit. Drive north on Angeles Crest Highway approximately 23 miles to Charlton Flats Picnic Area, and turn left (USFS road 3N16). Drive 1.4 miles, staying left at all forks, to a gate across a dirt road (the paved road will continue on to the right). Park here, careful not to block the locked gate.

HIKING
Walk around the gate and follow the dirt road to the summit of Vetter Mountain. There you will find a historic old fire lookout that was recently brought back into service.

HIKING VARIATION
There is a narrow use trail, which parallels the dirt road, that can be taken southeast from the summit along a ridge, back to the locked gate. The trail, which winds along the ridge through boulders, chaparral and pines, can be found behind some boulders just southeast of the summit.

NOTES
While you and your canine companion walk the dirt road to the summit, enjoy the smells of the Jeffrey and ponderosa pine, wild lilac and mountain mahogany. The 360-degree view of the San Gabriel Mountains from the summit is absolutely spectacular. Vetter Mountain was named in the 1930s for USFS Forest Ranger, Victor Vetter, who was a recipient of the USFS Bissell Medal for his work in forest conservation. The fire lookout on the summit of Vetter was built in 1930.

MT. HILLYER (6,200')
FROM THE SANTA CLARA DIVIDE ROAD

Rating: Easy
Recommended for: Out-of -shape and small well-conditioned dogs
Mileage: 300' of gain, 8 miles, 5.5 hours round-trip on fire road
K9 water: 1 quart, no water on route
Ambience: Peaceful trail through meadow and pines
Maps: Automobile Club of Southern California Los Angeles and Vicinity
Hiking maps: USGS Chilao Flat and Mt. Waterman 7.5 minute topos
Best time to hike: April to November. The Santa Clara Divide Road is often closed or blocked by snow during winter.

DRIVING

Take the 210-Fwy. to the 2-Angeles Crest Highway in La Canada and exit. Drive north on Angeles Crest Highway approximately 26.5 miles to the Santa Clara Divide Road (USFS road 3N17) and turn left. Drive 2.8 miles on the Santa Clara Divide Road, past the signed entrance to the USFS Horse Flats Campground, about 0.5 mile to a parking area on the left (west) side of the road. Walk to a dirt road just behind several wooden posts (no vehicle access to the dirt road).

HIKING

Walk south on the dirt road which eventually narrows to a trail. Follow the trail up a small, steep hill through open meadows sparsely forested with Jeffrey pine. The forest thickens and large, prominent boulders mark either side of the trail as it flattens out along the ridge to the summit. The summit of Mt. Hillyer is on the right (north) side of the trail, the highest mound of rocks. A post marks the spot.

NOTES

The trail to Mt. Hillyer is a pretty, peaceful trail shaded by pines off the beaten track and is a popular hike for families with small children. An occasional rock climber can be found bouldering on the rocks near the summit of the peak.

Named for Mary Hillyer (1865-1933) who worked for Angeles National Forest Supervisor William V. Mendenhall in the 1920s, the rocky outcrops of Mt. Hillyer and vicinity provided the perfect hideout for the bandito Tiburcio Vasquez (1835-1875) for whom Vasquez Rocks in Agua Dulce were named. Vasquez pastured his horses in the area known as Horse Flats just below Hillyer's summit.

MT. WILLIAMSON (8,214') FROM ANGELES CREST HIGHWAY

Rating: Strenuous
Recommended for: Well-conditioned dogs
Mileage: 1,600' of gain, 5 miles, 3-4 hours round-trip on trail
K9 water: 2 quarts, no water on route
Ambience: Beautiful views of San Gabriels, Mojave Desert and San Andreas Fault Zone
Maps: Automobile Club of Southern California Los Angeles and Vicinity
Hiking maps: USGS Crystal Lake 7.5 minute topo
Best time to hike: April to November. During a good snow year, Angeles Crest Highway is closed just past the Kratka Ridge ski area. Listed below are two alternate hike routes up Mt. Williamson, one from the west and one from the east, each accessed from different trailheads and parking areas along Angeles Crest Highway.

DRIVING ROUTE A

Take the 210-Fwy. to 2-Angeles Crest Highway in La Canada and exit. Drive north on Angeles Crest Highway approximately 38 miles to a large dirt parking area (about 2.5 miles past Kratka Ridge ski area) on the left (north) side of Angeles Crest Highway, about 0.5 miles before the first tunnel on the highway.

HIKING ROUTE A

From the east end of the parking lot, follow a dirt road about 100 yards to a trail and turn right (east). Follow this trail as it switchbacks up the southwest ridge of Mt. Williamson, through groves of Jeffrey and ponderosa pines. Approximately two miles up the trail, you reach the top of the ridge and the trail that comes up from Islip Saddle. From this point follow an obvious use trail north, crossing several bumps to the summit.

DRIVING ROUTE B

Take the 210-Fwy. to 2-Angeles Crest Highway in La Canada and exit. Drive north on Angeles Crest Highway approximately 39.5 miles to Islip Saddle. Turn left into, and park, in a paved parking area on the north side of Angeles Crest Highway.

HIKING ROUTE B

Start walking up the Pacific Crest Trail from the west end of the parking area. Follow the trail as it winds along the side of a mountain ridge which steepens steadily through open terrain, sparsely forested

CANINES AND THEIR PEOPLE ENJOYING THE SUMMIT OF MT. WILLIAMSON   PHOTO: JULIE RUSH

with pines and scrub. At the top of the ridge, turn right (northeast) on a use trail to the summit of Mt. Williamson, elevation 8,214'.

NOTES

Mt. Williamson was named after United States Army Lieutenant Robert Stockton Williamson who, in 1853, led a survey party charged with finding a suitable rail route across the San Gabriel Mountains. Williamson successfully located Cajon Pass and Soledad Pass.

From either route, this is a wonderful hike. From the summit, one can look out across the southern Mojave Desert. The boulder and rock out-croppings of the San Andreas Fault Zone can be seen running parallel along the base of the San Gabriel Mountains.

MT. LEWIS (8,396')

Rating: Moderate
Recommended for: Small, well-conditioned dogs
Mileage: 500' of gain, 1 mile, 1 hour round-trip on dirt road
K9 water: 1 quart, no water on route
Though not posted, on-leash recommended
Ambience: Views across the San Gabriels and Mojave Desert
Maps: Automobile Club of Southern California Los Angeles and Vicinity
Hiking maps: USGS Crystal Lake 7.5 minute topo
Best time to hike: April to November depending on snow. In winter, during a good snow year, Angeles Crest highway is closed just past the Kratka Ridge ski area.

DRIVING

Take the 210-Fwy. to the 2-Angeles Crest Highway in La Canada and exit. Drive north on Angeles Crest Highway approximately 44.5 miles to Dawson Saddle on the left (north) side of the highway, where there is a highway maintenance building. The name of the saddle is posted at the top of the building. Park.

HIKING

Just to the west side of the highway maintenance building is the use trail to the summit of Mt. Lewis. Follow it, as it climbs steeply to the top of the ridge, through groves of Jeffrey pine. At the top of the ridge, continue north to the summit of the peak.

NOTES

Mt. Lewis is a steep, short climb but well worth the spectacular views across the Mojave Desert and the north side of the San Gabriel Mountains. The peak was named after Washington "Dusty" Lewis, the first Superintendent of Yosemite National Park and Assistant Director of the National Park Service. As a topographer for the USGS, he worked in the San Gabriel Mountains from 1906 to 1919 and was widely known for his love of the wilderness. The summit of Mt. Lewis can be one of the most rarely traveled, peaceful locations in the San Gabriel Mountains

MT. BADEN POWELL (9,399')

Rating: Strenuous!!

Recommended for: Well-conditioned dogs only!!

Mileage: 2,800' of gain, 8 miles, 6 hours round-trip on trail

K9 water: 2-3 quarts minimum, no water on route (with the exception of the signed Lamel Spring, about 300 feet off the trail)

Though not posted, on-leash recommended

Ambience: Beautiful views to Mt. Baldy and across the San Gabriels

Maps: Automobile Club of Southern California Los Angeles and Vicinity

Hiking maps: USGS Crystal Lake 7.5 minute topo

Best time to hike: April to November depending on snow. In winter, during a good snow year, Angeles Crest highway is closed just past the Kratka Ridge ski area.

DRIVING

Take the 210-Fwy. to 2-Angeles Crest Highway in La Canada and exit. Drive north on Angeles Crest Highway approximately 46.9 miles to Vincent Gap, and a large parking area on the right (south) side of Angeles Crest Highway. Park.

HIKING

On the southwest side of the parking lot is a restroom, a trail sign

for Mt. Baden-Powell and other trails. Start the trail at the sign for Mt. Baden-Powell and follow it as it switchbacks up through pines and classic San Gabriel Mountain terrain to the summit.

NOTES

Knighted by King Edward VII in 1909, Lieutenant-General

CANINES ON THE SUMMIT OF MT. BADEN-POWELL

Robert Baden-Powell, born Robert Stephenson Smyth Powell, is credited with founding the world boy scout movement in 1908, predecessor to the Boy Scouts of America. The peak is named in his honor.

BIG HORN MINE FROM VINCENT GAP (6,565')

Rating: Easy-moderate
Mileage: 500' of gain, 4 miles, 2 hours round-trip on dirt road
K9 water: 1 quart, snow fed seeps and springs on route
Though not posted, on-leash recommended
Ambience: Views to Mt. Baly overlooking the Sheep Mountain Wilderness, walk to largest 1800s gold mine still standing in the San Gabriels
Maps: Automobile Club of Southern California Los Angeles and Vicinity
Hiking maps: USGS Mount San Antonio 7.5 minute topo
Best time to hike: April to November depending on snow. In winter, during a good snow year, Angeles Crest highway is closed just past the Kratka Ridge ski area.

DRIVING

Take the 210-Fwy. to the 2-Angeles Crest Highway in La Canada and exit. Drive north on Angeles Crest Highway approximately 46.9 miles to Vincent Gap, and a large parking area on the right (south) side of Angeles Crest Highway. Park.

HIKING

On the southwest side of the parking lot is a restroom, a trail sign (for Mt. Baden-Powell and other trails) and a locked gate, painted red and white. Take the dirt road on the other side of the locked gate (at the time of this writing, there was no trail sign marking this route up to the Big Horn Mine). Follow the road as it contours through tall pines across the lower slopes of Mt. Baden-Powell. Continue up the road as it gradually steepens. Nearing the top of the steep part, there is a road fork, marked by a six-foot tall post on the right. On either side of this post are old ruins and foundations of the turn-of-the-century mining camps. Continue on the road fork to the right, a short distance to the Big Horn Mine. There is a cold snow-fed spring at the end of the road, coming out of the closed mine. Recommend viewing the old mill site from this point. Return by the same route.

NOTES

An interesting note about the rock formations found around the Big Horn Mine. A combination of sea sediment and volcanics known as Pelona Schist, these rocks were first deposited millions of years ago in the desert area south of the Blythe, California near the Colorado River. Remarkably, they were transported to the San Gabriel Mountains by movement along the San Andreas Fault.

THE BIG HORN MINE

The Big Horn Mine, located in the Sheep Mountain Wilderness, was one of the largest gold mines in the San Gabriel Mountains, first prospected around 1895, by Charles Tom Vincent who lived in a cabin near Vincent Gulch. Unable to come up with the funds needed to run the mine, Vincent relinquished it to various promoters and mining companies who worked it intermittently over the next forty years or so.

The views along the trail to the Big Horn Mine are absolutely spectacular, across the deep canyon of the East Fork of the San Gabriel River to the dramatic peaks of the Mt. Baldy area. Mt. Baldy is often snow-capped in the months of April and May, and is a sight well worth seeing if you have the chance.

SUNSET PEAK (5,796')

Rating: Moderate
Mileage: 1,500" of gain, 7 miles, 3 hours round-trip on fire road
K9 water: 1-2 quarts, no water on route
Ambience: Excellent moderate hike, nice views
Maps: Automobile Club of Southern California Los Angeles and Vicinity
Hiking maps: USGS Mount San Antonio and Mt. Baldy 7.5 minute topos
Best time to hike: All-year. Can be hot June through September.

ON THE WAY TO SUNSET PEAK

DRIVING

Take Interstate-10 to Indian Hill Blvd. in Claremont and exit. Drive north 2.0 miles on Indian Hill to Foothill Blvd. Turn right (east) on Foothill Blvd. and drive approximately 1.0 mile to Mills Avenue. Turn left (north) on Mills Avenue and follow to Mt. Baldy Road where Mills Avenue begins to turn northeast. Follow the Mt. Baldy Road approximately 7.8 miles to Glendora Ridge Road, located just on the outskirts of Mt. Baldy Village (if you go all the way through the village, you've gone too far). Turn left on Glendora Ridge Road and drive approximately 1 mile to the large dirt parking area on the right, known as Cow Canyon Saddle.

HIKING

From the parking lot, walk south across the Glendora Ridge Road to a gated dirt road, somewhat hidden by chaparral. Walk the dirt road, as it parallels above the Glendora Ridge Road, while steadily climbing to the summit of Sunset Peak. There are two obvious forks on the dirt road. Stay left at each fork.

NOTES

A pleasant, gradual walk up a slope through pines to the summit.

THE SAN RAFAEL HILLS

Millions of years ago, the San Rafael and Verdugo Hills were attached to the San Gabriel Mountains, before earthquakes along the Sierra Madre Fault Zone pushed them to the front of the San Gabriel Range. The Crescenta Valley was created between the two ranges. Flint Peak, the highpoint of the San Rafael Hills "towers" above Cerro Negro (*pronounced Nay-gro*), meaning Black Hill in Spanish, by only two feet and is almost three thousand feet lower than the lofty summit of Mt. Lukens, the highest point within Los Angeles city limits.

The San Rafael Hills are bordered by the great canyon of the Arroyo Seco to the east, Eagle Rock to the south and the Verdugo Hills to the west. Fires have always been part of the natural environment, but devastating ones swept across the San Rafael Hills during the late nineteenth century and first half of the twentieth century. During the depression years, the Civilian Conservation Corps (CCC) built a fire road along the crest of the San Rafael Hills. Using burros, the CCC also helped the USFS build fire stations on top of Mt. Lukens and Mt. Gleason. When the work was done, the burros were pastured in the fields and foothills surrounding the Crescenta Valley.

In November of 1933, a massive fire believed to be the work of an arsonist, began in the San Gabriel foothills above Tujunga, and quickly swept across the ridges and canyons surrounding Mt. Lukens. The fire burned more than a thousand acres and was fought by nearly three thousand men. The ensuing winter rains created disastrous flooding from the Big Tujunga Wash to the Arroyo Seco and canyons east. At least four hundred homes were lost and thirty-four known people died. As a result of that fire, the United States Forest Service built fire lookouts on the summit of Cerro Negro in the San Rafael Hills and on Verdugo Peak in the Verdugo Mountains. The tower on the summit of Verdugo Peak has since been removed. Only the tower on Cerro Negro is still standing today, though it is no longer used as a fire lookout.

OLD FIRE LOOKOUT ON SUMMIT OF CERRO NEGRO (BLACK HILL)

CERRO NEGRO (BLACK HILL 1,887')

Rating: Easy
Recommended for: Well-conditioned dogs
Mileage: 400' of gain, 1.5 miles round-trip on fire road
K9 water: 1 quart, no water on route
Recommend: Pets on leash, clean up after your pet
Ambience: Nice views of Glendale, Verdugo Hills, and Mt. Lukens
Maps: Automobile Club of Southern California Los Angeles and Vicinity
Hiking maps: USGS Pasadena 7.5 minute topo
Best time to hike: All-year. Hike early morning or around sunset on cooler summer days.

DRIVING

From 101-Ventura Fwy. drive north on the 2-Glendale Fwy. Exit on Mountain Street in Glendale. Drive east on Mountain which turns into Camino San Rafael. Follow Camino San Rafael as it winds through a residential area 1.9 miles to two fire roads on left. The north fire road (on the right) is paved and will be the one to hike. Park in the street, careful not to block the gate.

HIKING

Walk up the paved fire road. The pavement ends about 500' from the gate. Go left at the first fork, passing by high power lines on the right. Pass homes on the right and continue on the fire road as it climbs uphill. Stay right at a second fork. The fire lookout will come into view. Follow road to fire lookout.

NOTES

The name "Cerro Negro" means Black Hill in Spanish. The San Rafael hills are east of the Glendale Freeway, south of La Canada-Flintridge, north of Eagle Rock and west of Pasadena. Much lower than the San Gabriel Mountains, their flora and fauna is similar, thought the effects of encroaching residential development can be seen. On a clear day, there are fabulous 360-degree views of the San Gabriel Mountains, La Crescenta Valley, Verdugo Hills, the Los Angeles Basin to the Pacific Ocean. An old civil defense horn is attached to the lookout tower. Volunteers from Jet Propulsion Laboratory's Amateur Radio Club keep the summit of Cerro Negro clear of brush all year long, especially during fire season. This area burned a few years ago during a fire that shut down the 2-Glendale Fwy. The vegetation is growing back and the views are still wonderful. Look for flowers in early spring.

CRESCENTA VALLEY PARK

THE VERDUGO HILLS

The Verdugo Mountains, or Verdugo Hills, were named for Corporal Jose Maria Verdugo, from Baja who, in 1784 was given the first land grant in California. As a reward for his loyal service to the King of Spain, Verdugo received 36,000 acres that came to be known as Rancho San Rafael, an area bounded on the east by the Arroyo Seco, on the west by what is now the city of San Fernando. The ranch included most of the Crescenta Valley, the San Rafael and Verdugo Hills and what would later become the townsites of Glendale, Eagle Rock, La Canada, Verdugo City, and Montrose. The San Rafael Hills on the east side of the 2-Glendale Freeway bear the name of Verdugo's original rancho.

When he retired from the army, Verdugo dedicated all of his time to the ranch, raising cattle, horses, sheep, mules and growing a variety of produce. He died in 1831, leaving all of his property to his daughter ,Catalina, and son, Julio. By the late 1870s, both had died. The land had been divided up among more than two dozen family members or sold to pay debts after Mexico ceeded California to the United States.

Of the ranchos built by the Verdugo family, only one has been preserved to present day, that of Corporal Jose Maria Verdugo's grandson, Teodoro. The adobe, located at 2211 Bonita Drive off Canada Blvd. and Opechee Way, is listed on the National Register of Historic Places. Near the home is a large beautiful oak tree, called "The Oak of Peace," the site where Jesus Pico and other "Californio" leaders of Mexican California decided to surrender to the American forces of John Fremont on January 11, 1847.

The Verdugo Mountains are separated from San Gabriels to the north by the Crescenta Valley and Sierra Madre Earthquake Fault Zone, one of the major fault zones in the Los Angeles Basin. Verdugo Peak, at 3,126', is the range high point and is reached by several fire roads that are waterless, shadeless and steep. The western and south facing slopes are dry, brushy chaparral country. Coyotes still brave this land island sandwiched between Interstate-5, the 210-Foothill Fwy., the 134-Ventura Fwy, and the 2-Glendale Fwy.

PRESERVATION OF THE VERDUGO LAND ISLAND

Not long ago, the Verdugos were ravaged by a huge fire that lit up the night skies above the cities of Glendale and Burbank and further reduced the critical habitat for struggling mammals locked forever on this tiny parcel of acreage within the City of Los Angeles. It is very important that the *hands-free method of leashing* be used here, not only to reduce the possibility of a canine encounter with a rattlesnake but to preserve, protect and not disturb the immediate habitat for native species. Right along the trails, birds are nesting, mammals have their burrows. Hands-free leashing is an excellent way to hike with your dog on all Southern California fire roads and trails.

CRESCENTA VALLEY PARK WALK THROUGH THE OAKS

Rating: Easy
Recommended for: All dogs
Mileage: Minimal gain, 1 mile, 30 minutes round-trip on wide trail
K9 water: 1 quart, water fountains on route, shaded, restrooms
Posted: Pets on leash, clean up after your pet
Ambience: Pretty walk through oaks, sycamores and meadows
Maps: Automobile Club of Southern California Los Angeles and Vicinity
Hiking maps: Trails are fairly obvious
Best time to hike: All year. Early morning and evenings on cooler summer days.

DRIVING

From the 210-Fwy. eastbound exit on Lowell and turn right (south) on Honolulu Avenue. Follow Honolulu to Dunsmore Avenue and the entrance to the park (next to the recreation center and public works yard). Park in the parking lot.

HIKING

From the parking lot follow the small foot bridge across the Verdugo Wash to large grassy fields. At this point, there is a trail off to the right that meanders through giant boulders strewn on either side of the path. Large oaks shade the trail further along, reminiscent of a medieval forest, truly Nottingham style, in the middle of Los Angeles. As you pass through the trees, there is an open field on the left that gently slopes up to beautiful oak trees and what appears to be a Sequoia, the only tree of its kind in the park. To the right of this field and past the "Sequoia" is a trail that traverses through a seasonal stream up into the wilds of the Verdugo Hills. This trail is uphill and will provide an excellent aerobic workout. Watch for poison oak, at its peak from spring to late fall.

Back out on our original trail, the road forks high and low. The lower half passes by a restroom and water fountain. The high trail passes through more oaks, rocks and woods.

At the end of this part of the park, return to your car or continue on to another fork. One trail parallels the Verdugo Wash where you can hear the sound of trickling water while the other trail weaves its way through sagebrush, oaks and wildflowers. During the summer, watch for rattlesnakes crossing the path. Keep your dog on leash to avoid an encounter in the tall grass.

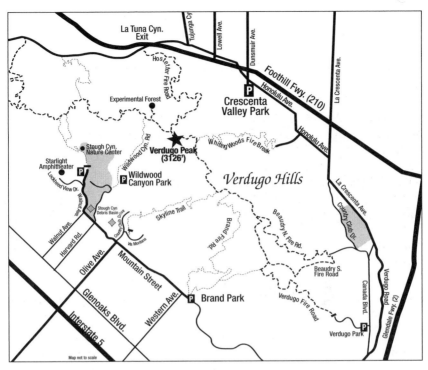

VERDUGO PEAK (3,126')

Rating: Strenuous!

Recommended for: Well-conditioned dogs!

K9 water: 2 quarts minimum

Posted: Pets on leash. Recommend cleaning up after your pet

Ambience: Oaks, sycamores and meadows in lower canyons. Spectacular view of high desert thunderheads over the San Gabriel Mountains from time to time. Steep, shadeless fire roads through dry brushy chaparral on higher ridges.

Warnings: Rattlesnakes, ticks

Maps: Automobile Club of Southern California Los Angeles and Vicinity

Hiking maps: USGS Burbank 7.5 minute topo

Best time to hike: November to early April

Whiting Woods to Verdugo Peak: 5.6 miles, 1,950' gain, 3-4 hours round-trip

DRIVING

210-Fwy. to Pennsylvania Ave. and exit. Turn south to Honolulu, turn left on Whiting Woods and follow to its end and park.

HIKING

From the end of Whiting Woods Road, walk past the locked gate. Follow the steep fire road approximately 2.4 miles to the Verdugo Fire Road, the fire road that runs along the crest of the range. Pleasant views of oaks and greenery are soon overshadowed by the steep push up the trail. At the top of the crest, turn right on Verdugo Fire

Road and head toward the radio towers. The high point of the range, Verdugo Peak is little less than a half mile from the top of Whiting Woods. Beautiful views.

Hostetter Fire Road to Verdugo Peak: 6.8 miles, 1,426' gain, 3-4 hours round-trip.

DRIVING

From the 2-Glendale Fwy. head west on the 210 Fwy. to La Tuna Canyon and exit. Turn left on La Tuna Canyon, passing under the freeway overpass. The parking area is on the left just past the overpass next to the eastbound on-ramp. Coming from the west, take the 210 to La Tuna Canyon and exit. At the end of the off-ramp, the parking lot is across the street, on the right side of the eastbound on-ramp.

HIKING

Pass through the locked gate on the east side of the parking area and follow the old concrete one lane road about 0.5 miles to a dirt road on your right, the Hostetter Fire Road. Follow fire road from La Tuna Canyon to the top of the highest ridge (toward the antennae) about 3.1 miles. When you reach the crest turn left on the Verdugo Fire Road. This road follows the crest of the range.

CAR SHUTTLE HIKING VARIATION

Leave one car at Whiting Woods, another car at Hostetter and hike one-way to Whiting Woods. There is an abundance of hiking opportunity in the Verdugo Hills, from traversing the range east to west, or crossing it north to south. Be prepared for long, adventuresome days.

NOTES

The Verdugos offer many aerobic and scenic hiking opportunities, but be prepared to hear the hum of the 210-Freeway on many of the trails. Thanks to the mountain bikers and folks walking their dogs, the Hostetter trail head gets a lot more foot traffic than it used to in the old days. La Tuna Canyon has always been a dumping ground for people to cheap to pay the fees to properly dispose of their trash at the landfill. The City has tried to keep it clean. Letters to your councilperson will remind them to take care of this area.

Hollywood Hills
WILACRE PARK TO COLDWATER CANYON
VIA THE BETTY B. DEARING TRAIL

Rating: Moderate
Recommended for: Well-conditioned dogs, all sizes
Mileage: 500' of gain, 2.5 miles, 1-2 hours round-trip on fire road
K9 water: 1-2 quarts, no water on route
Posted: Pets on leash, clean up after your pet
Ambience: Excellent moderate hike, nice views
Maps: Automobile Club of Southern California Los Angeles and Vicinity
Hiking maps: Trail is well marked
Best time to hike: November to April. Early morning and evenings on cooler summer days.

DRIVING

From the 101-Ventura Fwy. exit on Laurel Canyon Boulevard and drive south approximately 1.3 miles to Fryman Canyon Road. Turn right and park in the parking lot, the first driveway on the right. This trail is very popular and on any given weekend, you'll find a lot of cars parked in every direction. It is a residential neighborhood, so be careful not to park in front of someone's driveway. More than one ticket has been issued and a car towed for blocking a driveway.

HIKING

Walk up the paved driveway and follow the paved road as it gradually climbs up through the old cypress and jacaranda trees, to a plateau and the old foundation of what was once the estate home of Wil Acres, the cowboy movie star of silent motion picture fame. At this point, the pavement turns to a dirt fire road.

Continue up the fire road as it winds its way around ridges. There are great views across the San Fernando Valley to the San Gabriel Mountains on a clear day. Follow the fire road to a major fork, marked by a Santa Monica Mountains Conservancy sign. Take the right fork (west) to Coldwater Canyon. About a hundred yards from the fork, notice a stone stairway on the left. Follow this up a number of terraces to the TreePeople headquarters. If you miss the stairway, there is another one about a hundred feet down the trail in the direction of Coldwater Canyon. There are picnic tables, a restroom, a soda machine, and a faucet with a bucket beneath where

VIEW FROM WILACRE TRAIL OF VERDUGO HILLS AND MT. LUKENS

people like to water their dogs. There is a display on recycling and the local area, as well as a nature trail. The TreePeople headquarters are open Monday through Friday (call for hours). Return to Laurel Canyon by the same route, downhill almost all the way.

NOTES

This hike can be done in reverse order, from the TreePeople parking lot to Laurel Canyon, or you can continue on to Fryman Canyon Overlook farther up the hill on Mulholland Drive, but we don't recommend this route for dogs for a couple of reasons. First, when we scouted the trail, it was very overgrown, to the point that we were having to pick our way through the thick brush. Having grown up in the Studio City hills, the author remembers how many rattlesnakes we used to catch in our backyard, and the idea of not being able to see below one's knees isn't a comforting thought when hiking in rattlesnake territory. We prefer the open fire road to the overgrown trail since the visibility is much better.

The TreePeople is a non-profit group dedicated to tree-planting projects. Their headquarters are in the old Los Angeles County Fire Station 108, once famous for rescuing people who had the misfortune of driving their cars off Mulholland Drive. The trail was named for the late Betty B. Dearing, an environmental activist with the Santa Monica Mountains Conservancy.

FRANKLIN CANYON RANCH SITE

Rating: Varies, easy to strenuous
Recommended for: Out-of-shape, older or small dogs
Mileage: Varies
K9 water: 1 quart, there are water fountains
Posted: Pets on leash, clean up after your pet
Ambience: Pleasant walking around a lake through the cool shade of tall pines
Maps: Automobile Club of Southern California Los Angeles and Vicinity
Hiking maps: Trails are well marked. NPS maps available at site
Best time to hike: All-year. On cooler summer days, hike in early morning or before sunset

DRIVING

From the 101-Ventura Fwy. exit on Coldwater Canyon Boulevard and go south approximately 2.3 miles to Mulholland Drive. Turn right, not immediately onto Mulholland Drive West, but on the second street to the south, somewhat hidden by dense foliage. This is Franklin Canyon. Follow Franklin Canyon as it begins a winding descent through a residential neighborhood. At 0.2 mile, reach the park entrance. At 0.6 mile, turn left at fork with a sign noting the Sooky Goldman Nature Center. At 0.7 mile, there is a parking lot on the left. Park here to walk around the lake or down to the Wodoc Nature Trail, or continue another 0.2 of a mile to a small parking area (room for maybe four or five cars) on the right, with restrooms. Park here for the beginning of the Wodoc Nature Trail. To get to the Doheny Ranch, continue down the road which crosses at the south end of a reservoir and turn right at the stop sign. Follow the road 0.3 miles and turn left on Lake Drive. Follow this about a half mile to a parking lot on the left with restrooms. There is a beautiful, large grassy area with picnic tables.

From Sunset Blvd., on the westside, go north on Beverly Drive which turns into Coldwater Canyon. Follow to Mulholland heading west. At intersection of Coldwater and Mulholland West, turn left on Franklin Canyon Drive.

HIKING

This riparian area is filled with wildlife, including a variety of nesting birds, and is visited by families with small children, so it is important that pets are leashed. Pets are not allowed to swim in the

FRANKLIN CANYON

reservoirs which are used for drinking water. Canines frolicking in the water, upsets nesting wildlife.

Wodoc Nature Trail (0.1 mile): Easy nature trail, with interpretative signs identifying plants, that loops around Heavenly Pond (its real name), complete with a variety of ducks and a fountain. It is a favorite location for painting classes. Poopy scoop gloves are provided.

Chernoff Trail (0.6 mile): There are a number of different routes to take to walk around the lake. Some people just walk the road for ease. From the Wodoc Nature Trail, walk south along the paved road to the southeast end of the reservoir. Note the Cross Trail on the opposite side of road from this point. Follow the Chernoff Trail down along the water's edge, then walk through lush native and non-native plants. At the north end of the reservoir cross over to the west side (location depends upon height of water in reservoir) and continue around west side.

Cross Trail (0.7 mile, 200' gain): Cross Trail begins across the street from the southeast end of the reservoir as noted above. It climbs steeply for a short way, then essentially parallels Franklin Canyon, through coastal sage and chaparral. It ends at Franklin Canyon and Lake Drive. Walk another half mile down Lake Drive and the Doheny Ranch is reached.

FRANKLIN CANYON RESERVOIR

Hastain Trail (2.3 miles, 700' gain'): This is the most strenuous of the developed trails and starts just south of the ranch house on the east side of the lawn. Follow the trail as climbs steeply up a ridge, to an overlook with spectacular views out to the Pacific Ocean. From the overlook, follow the trail as it turns north (left) on the fire road and gently descends to the park entrance at Lake Drive.

NOTES

There are several other trails in Franklin Canyon and maps are usually available at trailside locations scattered around the park. The Doheny Ranch was one of six owned by the Doheny family, who made their fortune in the oil fields of Los Angeles around the turn of the century. The Spanish style house was built in 1935 at the north end of their four hundred acre Beverly Hills ranch and was used by the family as a weekend getaway. The upper Franklin Canyon reservoir was constructed in 1914 by the Los Angeles Department of Water and Power to store water transported down from the Owens Valley on the east side of the Sierra Nevada via the Los Angeles Aqueduct.

Sold to developers in 1977 who intended to build exclusive homes on the Doheny property, development was delayed for various reasons. The property was purchased by the National Park Service in 1981 for preservation of open space and the enjoyment of the public.

BONE - A - FIDO OFF-LEASH DOG PARKS!

When this book first came out in 1995 there were few off-leash dog parks. As open space vanishes in Los Angeles and Southern California the number of dog parks is on the increase. They are simple in concept and serve a great purpose for landlocked dogs: an open, fenced space protected from traffic where dogs can run freely to their hearts content.

Dog parks are not for everyone or every dog. There are some big dogs in the big dog section that might make one nervous and there are the tiniest little dogs in the small dog section. It takes awhile for a new dog who has never been in a dog park to get used to it. The pack mentality comes into play so it's important that dogs are socialized and owners pay attention to their behavior in the park. Leashes are left at the front gate. A leash on a dog when other dogs are off-leash puts the leashed dog on the defensive.

It is a great opportunity for owners to get together and socialize. At every dog park we visited, owners were gathered on lawn chairs and at picnic tables talking about their dogs.

THE GOLDEN RULES APPLY

Each park is governed by the "golden rules" listed below and offer separate areas for large and small dogs. Golden rules are as follows:

Owners must clean up after their dogs; dogs must be socialized; aggressive dogs are not allowed in the parks; maximum of three dogs per person; all dogs must be over four months old, licensed and vaccinated; dogs with communicable diseases and females in heat must be kept at home; dogs must be leashed outside the dog parks, in the parking lots or on the street.

Suggested Driving Maps: Automobile Club of Southern California Los Angeles and Vicinity and the Thomas Guide for Los Angeles and Orange Counties

HAPPY DOGS AT LAUREL CANYON DOG PARK

CALABASAS BARK PARK

CALABASAS BARK PARK 🐾 CALABASAS

Address: 4232 Las Virgenes Rd. Calabasas, CA 91302
Amenities: Benches, portable restroom, water, grass, shade
Warnings: Rattlesnakes, ticks, triple digits in summer
Maps: Automobile Club of Southern California Los Angeles and Vicinity

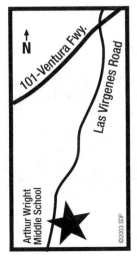

DRIVING:
101-Ventura Fwy. to Las Virgenes Road and exit. Drive south on Las Virgenes about 1.0 mile to Arthur E. Wright Middle School. The bark park is across the street on the left (east). Plenty of parking.

NOTES:
A lovely park on the edge of the chaparral in Santa Monica Mountains National Recreation Area. On the north corner of the park is a trail up to the top of the ridge just above the dog park, that overlooks Calabasas and Agoura. Watch for rattlesnakes and ticks in the tall grass.

RUBY

San Fernando Valley
SEPULVEDA BASIN OFF-LEASH DOG PARK 🐾 ENCINO

Address: 17550 Victory Blvd., Encino CA 91316
Amenities: Water, portable restrooms, baggies, shade, grass.
Fenced large and small dog areas.
Bring a lawn chair!
Hours: Sunrise to sunset Saturday-Thursday; Friday 11am to sunset
Maps: Automobile Club of Southern California Los Angeles and Vicinity

DRIVING:

101-Ventura Fwy. to White Oak Ave. exit in Encino. North on White Oak to Victory. Turn right on Victory. Turn into first driveway on the right, a long block down. Plenty of parking.

NOTES:

Located on the corner of White Oak Ave. and Victory Blvd. in the San Fernando Valley, this five acre plus fenced park is a safe and secure

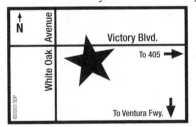

area where dogs can romp off-leash. It was the first park in the nation specifically developed for the purpose of letting dogs run off-leash. The Sepulveda Basin Dog Park Fund was established to let pet lovers make tax-deductible donations to be used for improvements and maintenance at the park. To become a supporter of the dog park, call (818) 785-5798.

SEPULVEDA BASIN OFF-LEASH DOG PARK LOOKING TOWARDS WHITE OAK

EDDY'S MEGAN ENJOYING THE EARTHY FRAGRANCES OF WHITNALL HIGHWAY DOG PARK

WHITNALL HIGHWAY OFF-LEASH DOG PARK
NORTH HOLLYWOOD

Address: Northwest corner of Cahuenga Blvd. and Whitnall Highway
Ambience: Water, shaded picnic tables, plastic lawn chairs, grass, portable restroom
Fenced large and small dog areas.
Maps: Automobile Club of Southern California Los Angeles and Vicinity

DRIVING:

From Toluca Lake, take Cahuenga Boulevard north to Whitnall Highway.
The park is on the northwest corner of Cahuenga and Whitnall Hwy.

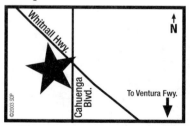

beneath the high power lines.

NOTES:

The City of Los Angeles did a nice job on this park planting pretty flowering trees, placing picnic tables, chairs and shade umbrellas. The park was very pleasant. Owners were all talking with each other while their dogs were having fun. Very nice view of the summer thunderheads over the San Gabriel Mountains.

Hollywood Hills
LAUREL CANYON OFF-LEASH DOG PARK

Address: 8260 Mulholland Drive, Studio City, CA 91604
Amenities: Water, portable restrooms, baggies, shade, grass.
Fenced large and small dog areas.
Hours: Sunrise to sunset. Closed Friday 7-11am for cleaning
Maps: Automobile Club of Southern California Los Angeles and Vicinity
To volunteer: laurelcynparkwatch.org

DRIVING FROM THE VALLEY:

From the 101-Ventura Fwy. take Laurel Canyon south to Mulholland.

Turn right (west) on Mulholland. At 0.2 miles look for the dog park sign on your left (south), a steep narrow driveway down to the parking lot. The dog park is below the street and not visible from Mulholland Drive.

DRIVING FROM HOLLYWOOD:

From Hollywood Blvd. take Laurel Canyon to Mulholland and turn left (west). At 0.2 miles look for the dog park sign on your left (south), a steep narrow driveway down to the parking lot. The park is not visible from Mulholland Drive.

NOTES:

This is a wonderful dog park, three lovely acres nestled in a beautiful little canyon with plenty of shade trees, picnic tables and portable restrooms.

RUNYON CANYON OFF-LEASH DOG PARK 🐾 HOLLYWOOD

Address: 2000 North Fuller Avenue, Hollywood, CA 90046
Amenities: 90 acres of unleashed dog territory all the way up to Mulholland Drive. Water, portable restrooms, baggies, shade, grass, trees, fire roads and trails. Fenced large and small dog areas. Play area for children.
Hours: Sunrise to sunset
Maps: Automobile Club of Southern California Los Angeles and Vicinity

DRIVING HOLLYWOOD ENTRANCE:
From Hollywood Blvd. turn north on Fuller Avenue. The park entrance is at the end of Fuller behind two large wooden gates. There

is also an entrance on North Vista Street. Try and find a parking spot along Franklin and be prepared to walk. There is no public parking lot and the street parking is hideous in Hollywood (and a lot of people don't clean up after their dogs).

DRIVING MULHOLLAND DRIVE:
There is an entrance up on Mulholland Drive about two miles west of the intersection of Cahuenga Blvd. and Mulholland Drive from the east, or about two miles east of Laurel Canyon from the west. Look for the dirt parking area on the south side of Mulholland.

NOTES:
Runyon Canyon is popular and very crowded. There is no public parking lot, only street parking on the Hollywood side. The Mulholland entrance (the dirt parking lot on the south side of Mulholland about two miles east of Laurel Canyon Blvd.) is better, but like the Grand Canyon, the hiking is all downhill. You have to walk back up again! It is a nice location for the folks who live in Hollywood and don't have to contend with parking.

Los Angeles
SILVERLAKE RECREATION AREA

Address: 1850 Silverlake Blvd. at Van Pelt Place
Ambience: Water, portable restrooms, baggies, shade, grass.
Fenced large and small dog areas.
Maps: Automobile Club of Southern California Los Angeles and Vicinity

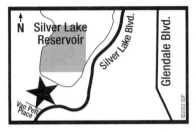

DRIVING:

Located on the south end of Silverlake Reservoir on Silverlake Boulevard a little over a mile from the intersection of Glendale and Silverlake Blvds. A small stretch of grass that provides a place for pets to play in a crowded urban environment, is a favorite haunt of all sizes and shapes of dogs especially on the weekends.

Venice Beach
WESTMINSTER OFF-LEASH DOG PARK

Address: 1234 Pacific Avenue, Venice, CA 90291
Amenities: Water, palm trees, benches, poop scoops, eucalyptus bark and dirt.
Fenced large and small dog areas.
Hours: Sunrise to sunset
Maps: Automobile Club of Southern California Los Angeles and Vicinity

DRIVING:

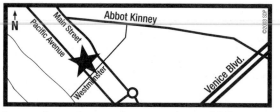

Take the 405 to the Venice Blvd. exit. Go west on Venice Blvd. to Pacific Avenue. Turn right (northwest) on Pacific. The park is located on the northeast corner of Westminster Avenue and Pacific behind the Senior Center. Parking is tight on adjacent streets but is permitted at the Senior Center after 3pm.

NOTES:

Venice Beach is only a block away. The dogs in this park were super mellow the day we visited. When a new dog came in, none of the other canines bothered to check out the new visitor. The neighborhood is more upscale than it was twenty years ago though still as quirky as ever.

KOKO LIKES THE WESTMINSTER DOG PARK

South Bay
EL SEGUNDO OFF-LEASH DOG PARK

Address: 600 E. Imperial Avenue, El Segundo, CA 90245
Amenities: Water, plastic lawn chairs, baggies, grass, dirt, nicely shaded.
Fenced large and small dog areas.
Hours: Sunrise to sunset
Maps: Automobile Club of Southern California Los Angeles and Vicinity

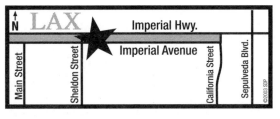

DRIVING:
Take the 105-Imperial Hwy. west to its end. Continue straight on Imperial Hwy.. to Main Street. Turn left (south) on Main, then make a quick left on Imperial Avenue heading east to Sheldon Street. The park is on left (north) side just past Sheldon.

NOTES:

Lovely little park in the shade on the green strip of land separating the two Imperials, known as Imperial Parkway. Fabulous view of the LAX runways here. People set up lawn chairs along Imperial Avenue (south of and parallel to Imperial Hwy.) just to watch the 747s.

HAPPY EL SEGUNDO DOG PARK CUSTOMER

REDONDO BEACH OFF-LEASH DOG PARK

Address: 200 Flagler Street, Redondo Beach, CA 90277
Amenities: Water, baggies, primarily dirt. Fenced large and small dog areas.
Bring a lawn chair!
Hours: Sunrise to 9pm. Closed Wednesday until noon for cleaning.
Maps: Automobile Club of Southern California Los Angeles and Vicinity

DRIVING:

Take the 405 south or north to the Inglewood Blvd. exit. Take Inglewood south to 190th Street. Go right (west) on 190th to the four-

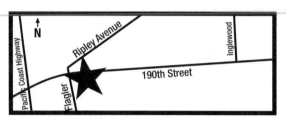

way stop intersection of Ripley-Flagler and 190th. Turn left on Flagler beneath the big electrical power lines. About 1/4 block, turn left into the public parking lot. The dog park is huge with large areas for small and big dogs.

NOTES:

Well-attended on weekends by Manhattan, Hermosa and Redondo

Beach families with their high energy dogs. When we were there, the big and small dogs, separated by the fence between their respective areas were racing each other back and forth along the fence. If the high energy is too much to take, especially for first time guests, there is a nice on-leash park with walking paths right next to the fenced dog park.

KNOLL HILL OFF-LEASH DOG PARK ⁂ SAN PEDRO

Address: Knoll Drive, San Pedro CA 90731
Amenities: Water, plastic lawn chairs, baggies, eucalyptus bark, nicely shaded. Fenced large and small dog areas.
Hours: Sunrise to sunset
Maps: Automobile Club of Southern California Los Angeles and Vicinity

DRIVING:
Take the 110-Harbor Fwy. south to Front Street, the cruise ship terminal exit. Turn left on Front. Look on the left side of the road for the very non-descript Knoll Drive, a one-way road. You'll see the one-way exit first. Take the second Knoll Drive driveway. If you reach Pacific Avenue, you've gone too far.

NOTES:
This was KoKo's first dog park and it was a good experience. It is a beautiful location overlooking the Los Angeles Harbor. Above the traffic and noisy street, it is the quietest of the dog parks. The folks who got this park going should pat themselves on the back! To find out more or to join, contact: Peninsula Dog Parks, Inc, P.O. Box 1937, San Pedro, CA 90733 or call (310) 514-0338.

KNOLL HILL OVERLOOKS THE LOS ANGELES HARBOR

BIBLIOGRAPHY

Belzer, Thomas J., Roadside Plants of Southern California, Mountain Press Publishing Co., Missoula, 1984

California Department of Fish and Game, Living with California Mountain Lions, California Department of Fish and Game, Sacramento, CA 1995

Carew, Harold D., History of Pasadena and the San Gabriel Valley, S.J. Clark Co, Pasadena, CA 1930

Cotton, Shires and Associates, Inc., Technical Review Geological/Geotechnical Data: Abalone Cove Landslide and Zone 2 Areas, September 12, 2001

Gray, Mary Taylor and Clarke, Herbert, Watchable Birds of California, Mountain Press Publishing Co., Missoula, 1999

Harrison, Tom, Trail Map of the Santa Monica Mountains, (Central and West)

Tom Harrison, San Rafael, CA 1993

Heil, Grant W., The Ventura County Historical Quarterly, Vol. XXI, No. 3, Ventura County Historical Society, Thousand Oaks, CA 1976

Lombard, Sarah R., Rancho Tujunga: A History of Sunland/Tujunga, Sunland Woman's Club, California 1990

London, Jack, The Call of the Wild and Other Stories, Grosset & Dunlap, New York 1965

McAuley, Milt, Hiking Trails of the Santa Monica Mountains, Canyon Publishing Co., Canoga Park, CA 1991

Miller, Frances Trevelyan, Byrd's Great Adventure, The John C. Winston Company, Philadelphia, PA 1930

Muir, John, Stickeen: The Story of a Dog, Houghton Mifflin Company, New York 1916

Pomona Valley Humane Society, Living with Wildlife, Pomona Valley Humane Society, Pomona, CA 1995

Quirarte, Louis, Summit Signatures, Hundred Peaks Lookout, Sierra Club, Los Angeles, CA 1990

Robinson, John W., Trails of the Angeles, Wilderness Press, Berkeley, CA 1971

Rusho, W.L., Everett Ruess: A Vagabond for Beauty, Peregrin Smith Books, Salt Lake City, Utah 1983

Security Trust and Savings Bank First of the Ranchos: The Story of Glendale, 1924

Sherer, John Calvin, History of Glendale and Vicinity, 1922

Steinbeck, John, Travels with Charley, The Viking Press, New York 1962

United States Department of Agriculture, Angeles National Forest Rules and Regulations, Forest Service Pacific Southwest Region, USDA 1992

United States Department of the Interior, Santa Monica Mountains National Recreation Area Eastern & Western Section maps, National Park Service 1993

INDEX

WWW.SPOTTEDDOGPRESS.COM   ORDER FORM

SPOTTED DOG PRESS.

Mail to:
Spotted Dog Press
P.O. Box 1721
Bishop CA 93515
800-417-2790
FAX 760-872-1319

Name:		
Address:		
City	State	Zip Code
Daytime Phone:		
Credit card #:		Exp. Date:
Signature		

Title	Price	Quantity	Total
High & Wild Galen Rowell HARD COVER 224 full color pages. Considered to be Galen Rowell's best mountain writing and photography. 23 new stories. A beautiful work. Hard cover with dust jacket.	**$34.95**		
Close Ups of the High Sierra II Norman Clyde 176 pages. NEW EDITION 2004. A new edition of Norman Clyde's writings.	**CALL!**		
Climbing Mt. Whitney Benti & Wheelock 80 pages. Information on permits, route descriptions, how to hike Whitney as a dayhike, backpack, moonlight hike or rock climb. Everything you need to know to get to the top of the highest peak in the contiguous U.S.	8.95		
Death Valley to Yosemite: Frontier Mining Camps and Ghost Towns Belden & DeDecker 192 pages. The most complete work available today on the mining camps from the Mojave Desert to the High Sierra. Beautifully written by two exceptional authors with detailed maps showing locations.	14.95		
Desert Summits: A Climbing & Hiking Guide to California and Southern Nevada Andy Zdon 418 pages. Definitive guide to the highpoints of California's and Southern Nevada's desert ranges from the Great Basin to the Mexican border.	19.95		
Favorite Dog Hikes in and Around Los Angeles Benti 160 pages. The best-selling trail guide to the dog trails of Los Angeles. With a pattern for making dog hiking boots.	12.95		
Grand Canyon Treks Harvey Butchart 288 pages. Butchart walked, air mattressed and climbed more than 12,000 miles in the Grand Canyon backcountry and is considered the leading authority.	16.95		
Out From Las Vegas Florine Lawlor 288 pages. Guide to more than sixty adventures within a day's drive of Las Vegas by newspaper and travel reporter, Las Vegas native, Florine Lawlor.	16.95		
Born Free and Equal Ansel Adams HARD COVER 128 pages. New edition written and photographed by Adams from 1943-1944 at Manzanar War Relocation Center. His most important social work.	45.00		
The Secret Sierra David Gilligan 288 pages. Explore the hidden world of the Sierra Nevada's alpine zone through the eyes of a naturalist.	18.95		
	Subtotal		
UPS Shipping $4.00 all orders!			
CA residents please add 7.25% sales tax **7.25% CA Sales Tax**			
Make check or money order payable to: Spotted Dog Press, P.O. Box 1721, Bishop, CA 93515-1721 **Total**			